GOVERNANCE
in the
NEW GLOBAL DISORDER

GOVERNANCE *in the* NEW GLOBAL DISORDER

Politics for a Post-Sovereign Society

DANIEL INNERARITY

Translated by
SANDRA KINGERY

Foreword by
SASKIA SASSEN

Columbia University Press   *New York*

Columbia University Press
Publishers Since 1893
New York   Chichester, West Sussex
cup.columbia.edu
Copyright © 2016 Columbia University Press
All rights reserved

Library of Congress Cataloging-in-Publication Data
Names: Innerarity, Daniel, 1959– author. |
Kingery, Sandra, 1964– translator.
Title: Governance in the new global disorder :
politics for a post-sovereign society / Daniel Innerarity ;
translated by Sandra Kingery ; foreword by Saskia Sassen.
Description: New York : Columbia University Press, 2016. |
Includes bibliographical references and index.
Identifiers: LCCN 2016018541| ISBN 9780231170604
(cloth : alk. paper) | ISBN 9780231542258 (e-book)
Subjects: LCSH: International cooperation. |
Globalization. | Sovereignty.
Classification: LCC JZ1318 .I5552 2016 |
DDC 306.2—dc23
LC record available at
https://lccn.loc.gov/2016018541

Columbia University Press books are printed on permanent
and durable acid-free paper.
Printed in the United States of America

c 10 9 8 7 6 5 4 3 2 1

Cover design: Martin N. Hinze
Cover image: © baona/iStockphoto

CONTENTS

Foreword by Saskia Sassen vii
Introduction: Whose World Is It? xi

PART I. AN UNPROTECTED WORLD

1 The Return of Pirates in the Global Era 3
2 Humanity Threatened 29

PART II. THE UNFULFILLED PROMISE OF PROTECTION

3 Global Fear 51
4 A Walled World 68

PART III. GOVERNING, OR THE ART OF TAKING CHARGE

5 The Observation Society 83
6 From Sovereignty to Responsibility 105
7 Climatic Justice 122

8 A Politics of Humanity 140
Epilogue: Us and Them 161

References 193
Index 203

FOREWORD

SASKIA SASSEN

In this passionate and original book, Daniel Innerarity unsettles a range of typical or familiar contrasts. In this process he repositions the familiar as part of a new interpretation. Nothing is left standing where it once stood. Key categories are evicted from their conventional anchors. But it is an eviction that entails making new meanings.

As I read through this book, there was one image that kept recurring in my mind, albeit not one used by the author—it was more my applying Innerarity's method to some of my work. The image is that the immigrant *makes* new ground for her mobility, and thereby makes identity into a practice. Here are meanings that keep rolling, not one can stand on its own in isolation: the moment it is uttered, it generates another meaning, in a sequence that eventually puts the reader in a faraway place from where the sentence, the paragraph, the page, or the chapter started. It is not analytical anarchy, but rather analytic freedom—concepts take on nomadic meanings that keep mutating.

But these mutating meanings can also become frightening. Innerarity asks: "How should we conceive of and govern a world made up of common threats and borderless sovereignties?

How should we protect ourselves in limitless spaces, in a world of nets, fluidity, and connections?" A beginning of an answer is that we must find "a grammar" that helps us see that there is no exclusive ownership, that what belongs to us is not necessarily exclusively so. . . . The privileged may think they can withdraw from dangers, but they cannot.

In a moment of practical observation, Innerarity argues that we cannot produce safety, and we should not promise it. Rather, "we can only offer cooperative solutions, projects for greater integration, and complex forms of justice for which there are barely models or precedents." Which brings him to what is probably his core argument, call, or thesis, that "what unifies us and puts us on equal footing is none other than the community of our threats, the shared risks that make it physically impossible to escape danger on our own." He tells us that we can illustrate these "harsh new conditions" with such conditions as the gaseous world, universal exposure, or "a world without outlying areas." Each of these images points toward "a shared vulnerability, a similar lack of protection, impossible immunity. The flip side of interdependence is common fragility and the fear of contagion." He posits that this is why "a reasonable cultivation of fear and the management of global risks are among the most important functions of today's governments, constituting a new opportunity for political innovation."

Innerarity's answer to many of the conundrums he examines is probably well captured in the following statement: "What we could call the civilizing of globalization is nothing but the reinvention of politics on a global scale in such a way that the world stops having owners and moves toward becoming a space for the citizenry."

Yet at the same time, in his relentlessly critical rather than romantic perspective, he also detects trajectories that might go in less attractive directions. Thus he posits that our maps of the world today no longer show a "coherent and complete collective of self-sufficient units, but an incomplete map, with areas of ambiguous sovereignty, spaces that are difficult to regulate, and hazy responsibilities." Again, here I see Innerarity executing that language operation that recurs relentlessly, to wit, that nothing is simply what it is.

In short, the play of metaphors proposed by the author as a way of examining today's world helps clarify a range of complexities. It throws light on emergent patterns that are easily experienced as intractable.

INTRODUCTION

Whose World Is It?

TODAY'S world is full of paradoxes, many of which could be summarized by the idea that it is a world belonging to everyone and to no one. There are many issues that are everyone's (they affect all of us and demand coordinated actions), but at the same time, no one can or wants to be in charge of them (either there is no competent authority or no one shoulders the responsibility). What is the difference between something held in common and something that is ungovernable, between shared responsibility and generalized irresponsibility? How do we distinguish that which belongs to everyone and that which belongs to no one, that which has no owner and that which is simply ignored? Are we not calling the void universal or celebrating as an "opening" that which is, in reality, simply vulnerability and a lack of protection?

This ambiguity is reflected in the opposing assessments with which we receive new realities. We declare the death of experts, the accessibility of information, the apotheosis of transparency, and the defeat of the need for mediation, but these very triumphs are also accompanied by the fear of deregulation, ungovernability, and opacity. Society is divided between optimists and pessimists, which is the axis on which we place ourselves when we have no idea of what is going on. Given this ambivalent perspective, who can assure us that everything we are now facing portends great success, rather than opening the doorway to disaster?

I propose we understand this new constellation—the dialectic between everyone and no one—as the condition that explains what we could, without metaphoric exaggeration, call the return of piracy in the global era. There is always piracy when new realities appear and it is not clear to whom they belong or where the competition lies. It makes sense that with the increase of universal public goods—such as the climate, security, knowledge, or financial stability—there has also been growing uncertainty about their possession and management. The timid configuration of humanity as the subject and agent of appeals converts what used to be sovereign states, landowners, or unilateral actors eo ipso into pirates. The current fluidification of property corresponds with the weakening of political sovereignty in a world of interdependencies; both phenomena stem from and share the same reality. World cartography no longer establishes a coherent and complete collective of self-sufficient units, but an incomplete map, with areas of ambiguous sovereignty, spaces that are difficult to regulate, and hazy responsibilities. All of this forces us to articulate a new state of equilibrium between the state, the marketplace, and society.

What unifies us and puts us on equal footing is none other than the community of our threats, the shared risks that make it physically impossible to escape danger on our own. These harsh new conditions can be illustrated with metaphors such as the gaseous world, universal exposure, or a world without outlying areas. Each of these images points toward a shared vulnerability, a similar lack of protection, impossible immunity. The flip side of interdependence is common fragility and the fear of contagion. That is why a reasonable cultivation of fear and the management of global risks are among the most important functions of today's governments, constituting a new opportunity for political innovation. Epidemic societies need agreements about acceptable risk, strategies that will protect them in the face of their own irrationality, which is clearly seen in phenomena such as financial crises, the side effects of technologies, or the management of security.

How should we conceive of and govern a world made up of common threats and borderless sovereignties? How should we protect ourselves in limitless spaces, in a world of nets, fluidity, and connections? We must learn a new grammar that conjugates that which belongs to us and that which belongs to other people as realities that are not necessarily opposed. We must understand that certain demands for security destroy the hope of converting danger into a source of a new cosmo-politics, in other words, into the consciousness of belonging to the same world. These security demands can, instead, lead certain societies (those that are most privileged) to withdraw from the collective world, shielding themselves from its dysfunctions. Rather than promising safety that is impossible to deliver, we can only offer cooperative solutions, projects for greater integration, and complex forms of justice for which there are barely models or precedents.

In a world in which the economy is largely deterritorialized and interdependencies aggravate our common vulnerability, there is no solution except movement toward global governance and a denationalization of justice. This would mean overcoming the incomplete integration of a world that is unified through technologies, the economy, and even certain cultural products and styles but that is particularly uneducated when it comes to its political and legal articulation. Common public goods—the mutual exposure to global risks regarding security, food, health, finances, or the environment—require a corresponding politics of humanity. What we could call the civilizing of globalization is nothing but the reinvention of politics on a global scale in such a way that the world stops having owners and moves toward becoming a space for the citizenry.

GOVERNANCE
in the
NEW GLOBAL DISORDER

PART I

AN UNPROTECTED WORLD

1

THE RETURN OF PIRATES
IN THE GLOBAL ERA

IN his famous book *The History of Piracy*, Philip Gosse (1989 [1932], 298) recalls that people, at the end of the nineteenth century, believed the disappearance of pirates was imminent. It was the dream of a world where there is no territory without sovereignty, in other words, no one distanced from the rules of the state (Thompson 1994; Anderson 1997). Subsequent history seems to flatly disprove this prediction. Piracy has stopped being a historical curiosity or a simple metaphor. Pirates are among us and taking on diverse forms in many different realms: pirates of the air and seas, radio pirates, parliamentary pirates, global terrorists, computer pirates and hackers, viruses, spam, illegal immigrants, squatters, biopiracy, lobbyists, free riders, financial pirates, leaks, data aggregators, flags of convenience, international organized crime, money laundering, and so on.

The pirate is part of the contemporary social imaginary of globalization, where there is a convergence of predatory capitalism, fundamentalist movements, networks that escape the states, and the libertarians of deregulated cyberspace. Piracy maintains a close relationship with the figure of the parasite since pirates cannot exist without a social system off of which they live, but to which they do not want to belong: viruses live off our organism; those who steal intellectual property are dependent on the existence of cultural creation; the financial economy depends in the end on what we call the real economy; and so on. There are also "free riders": people, institutions, or countries that go it alone and escape the agreements that should bind them.

The theme of piracy affords an interesting lens with which to consider many of our current conflicts regarding the ways in which ideas and technologies are created, distributed, and utilized. What is at stake, in the end, is the nature of the relationship we would like to maintain between creativity and commerce. It is not going too far to affirm that we are in the midst of the most profound revolution in intellectual property since the middle of the eighteenth century, and that it will probably destroy the conception of intellectual property that we have held until now and that is at the heart of our systems of copyrighting and patenting. Adrian Johns has announced this transformation by specifically taking the idea of piracy as a metaphor (Johns 2009). Internet protocols, in particular, seem to confirm that there are viable alternatives to the norms of traditional property. Many new business models make use of open software, which exploits previously unprecedented network properties; protests are being extended to the abuse of the system of pharmaceutical patents; and so on. In any case, the questions at stake do not merely represent changes in technology.

By virtue of the information economy, piracy has been generalized as a metastasis challenging the capacity to understand and control it. The accusation of piracy has turned into the reproach of our age, an omnipresent element in the discussions of business politics. At the same time as piracy has grown and diversified, a counterindustry dedicated to fighting it has also emerged.

The ambiguity of the phenomenon sparks very diverse reactions. The most fearful among us will fretfully affirm that we are moving toward a world full of pillage and plunder; on the other hand, the panorama seems to promise new emotions to those who are bored with the traditional political scene. In any case, it is worth asking if this reappearance of piracy gives us a clue to better understand the current world, its promises, and its dangers. We should verify the hypothesis that piracy is inseparable from the globalization of mercantile flows, from the formation of a transatlantic maritime world; that is why pirates are found in every period of transition. They have reappeared, in our case, given the current lack of definition about the nature and management of humanity's common goods in the context of globalization and the knowledge society. Whether in the Mediterranean during the seventh century, in the Atlantic beginning in the seventeenth century, or in its current form everywhere, the tactic of piracy always consists in lying in ambush as close as possible to mercantile flows and as far as possible from the large political-military centers. It is no longer necessary to move anywhere to be in a place like this since the reality of globalization is that the financial system prevails over the political system everywhere; all locations today are close to the economic networks and far from political power.

The current profusion of various types of piracy is a sign of the type of world we inhabit thanks to globalization; some scholars have interpreted this as a "liquid" world. With the increase in what we could call common public goods (the climate, Internet, health, security, financial stability, and so on), uncertainty about their ownership and management also increases. All the efforts to regulate these new realities could be understood as attempts to afford a certain territorial intelligibility to areas where a special ambiguity has reigned until now. The difficulty of the matter consists in that this can no longer be done within the old categories of the nation-state; it requires a new way of thinking and managing the new public space.

LAND AND SEA

The point of departure for this inquiry could be the divergence between the land and the sea that has been part of our geopolitical imaginary since Thucydides (1972), who contrasted coastal Athens to landlocked Sparta, one democratic and the other a conservative alliance. The premodern world was an imperial, "maritime" world, not organized on the basis of strict territoriality, as nation-states in the modern era would later be defined. Herman Melville, the great poet of the maritime world, has one of his characters in *Moby Dick* declare: "Noah's flood is not yet subsided." Both the unity and the division of the planet then depended on maritime factors. The empires wanted to assert their authority as hegemonic powers across the oceans. The imperial age cannot be understood without hydropolitics.

The legal notion of "territory," fixed and delimited, on the other hand, is a creation of modernity. The ancient world was still too fluid and limitless. Ancient and medieval cities and republics established dominion over specific geographic extensions. Even the Roman Empire admitted that its supremacy extended to the *Limes* of the empire. But this boundary was not a border. It was a point where the area of a specific jurisdiction stopped, a point provisionally reached by the advance of the legions. Even when they became stable, these were not strict limits. Instead, it was a zone of transition, commerce, and communication between the Roman and the barbarian worlds. There were typically these types of spaces in medieval cities. They were not divided by lines, but by areas, sometimes sufficiently broad so as to allow enclaves and exclaves, where authority could always be debated. In a strict sense, the line of territorial demarcation emerged much later. As many historians have shown, the border was an invention of the absolutist state, especially in France.

Sea and land are also confronted as images with epistemological meaning. In a famous passage from the *Critique of Pure Reason*, Kant contrasts solid land, which he calls the "land of truth," with the ocean as the "region of illusion" where the fog banks seem "a new country" (1968b, B294/A235). Modernity is epistemologically inaugurated as a supremacy of territorial permanence in the face of the fluidity and ambiguity of marine liquid.

Modernity is politically translated into the shape of the nation-state, based on territory, which establishes a new way of dividing the space of power, with clear jurisdictions and without areas of ambiguous sovereignty. But this period is a moment in history that is overcome in the middle of the twentieth century, when the process we call globalization is accentuated. The resulting interdependencies seem to lead us to a space that has more in common with the maritime indetermination of empire than with the solid ground of states.

The contrast between the sea and land also allows for a more general consideration of political theory in which two ways of understanding the social order become imaginarily opposed. Looking at things from this contrastive lens, we find this very antagonism in reflections made by Carl Schmitt in the period between the world wars (Schmitt 2008). The German jurist found it unfortunate that the dry-land nations, protectors of security and property, were growing weaker in the face of the maritime, liberal, oceanic powers. For Schmitt, the sixteenth and seventeen centuries were torn asunder by the antagonism between the terrestrial powers of closed societies and the maritime powers of open societies. This outline is the backdrop for all the political debates of modernity, which have revolved around a fundamental distinction between autarchic terrestrial states and limitless maritime powers, the collision between a political philosophy of land and a political philosophy of the sea, between a belief in limitation and a belief in limitlessness. For Schmitt, a conservative, that which is finite and completed represents the ideal, in contrast to that which is open and incomplete, typical of liberal societies. The supremacy of politics was symbolized for him in the power of solid ground, in the determination of that which is continental.

What horrified Carl Schmitt was that the land could collapse into the sea, in other words, that nations could end up disbanded in the ambiguity of a common public law. That explains his strong opposition to the birth of a new international order or jurisdiction, as he pointed out after the Second World War. Since then, the very dynamic of globalization has led us to the configuration of new spaces that require a jurisdiction beyond the national state, the appropriate management of interdependent common goods, and global governance. "Humanity" is now an inevitable term; from discussions about human rights and crimes against humanity to humanitarian associations and interventions, the name of our common species is crucial to refer to particular issues that point toward a cosmopolitan horizon.

This antagonism between the open sea and the limited land is very well exemplified in the philosophies of Grotius and Hobbes. The first is the defender of a world without static sovereignties and, therefore, without stable properties. Hobbes, on the other hand, is the champion of the terrestrial order.

We should recall the history that gave birth to this particular ideological juxtaposition. In 1603 in the Straits of Malacca, a Portuguese ship was captured by a ship belonging to the Dutch East India Company. Portugal denounced this act of piracy and demanded the restitution of its cargo, while the Dutch company tried to justify the seizure. The Dutch then appealed to Hugo Grotius, a young lawyer at that point, who argued, in a work titled *De Jure Praedae Commentarius* (1606), that it was an act of legitimate defense against a country, Portugal, that was trying to gain exclusive control over the Asian seas to guarantee their business. His final argument was that, in the name of natural rights, no one can appropriate the air or the water and that it is impossible to appropriate the sea, because it belongs to everyone.

In this way, Grotius justified the right to plunder, to appropriation, as the new maritime way of thinking. He questioned the sovereign states' attempts to appropriate the seas. Grotius came to affirm that the uninhabitable oceans had a specific legal status that made them closer to the properties of air. It was not possible to acquire fixed sovereignty over these elements. All attempts at possessing the open seas, whether they were claimed as a "discovery," through papal bulls, or through the laws of war or conquest, were equally invalid. A similar argument was formulated by that great writer of the seas, Herman Melville, who established a distinction in order to legitimize colonial capture between the "fast-fish," which belonged to stable, consolidated authorities, and the "loose-fish," which were fair game for whoever arrived first. He concluded that the "loose-fish" category included America for Columbus, Poland for the czars, and India for the English. There is also an old tradition that associates property with the cultivation of land and believes that what is not cultivated or not cultivatable (such as the sea) cannot strictly belong to anyone.

Plutarch once described the inhabitants of a certain island as pirates because they did not know how to cultivate the land. It is the same argument that was used to say that the Americas were unpopulated when the conquistadors arrived. Inhabiting means cultivating the land; those who do not do so do not have any rights over the space. That is why it was permissible to expel the indigenous peoples in the Americas or to freely ply the seas.

Hobbes's *Leviathan* (published in 1651) could be interpreted specifically as the attempt to establish terrestrial order and security against maritime disorder. The modern nation-state thus arose against the disorder of the sea, against that which is mobile, unstable, floating, fluctuating, and elusive, symbolically personified by pirates. It is not surprising, therefore, that Schmitt found in Hobbes a precedent for his conception of a sovereign state, as that which introduces order and limitations in the face of maritime chaos.

THE NEW ECONOMY OF PILLAGING

Everything seems to indicate that the battle is currently tipped in favor of what Zygmunt Bauman has called the "liquid world" (2007): globalization is driven by general fluidity, which implies liquidation not only of the old borders, but also of the very idea of the border, which becomes obsolete in a deterritorialized space. We can comprehend what is going on with the metaphor of an "oceanification of the world," in which fluidity is liberated from territorial constriction. It is a question of a world in which displacement and flexibility are the only reality, a world of generalized circulation, in which everyone navigates, whether it is through digital, financial, or communicative spaces. What has not been fulfilled is Virgil's dream where, in the fourth of his *Eclogues*, he affirmed that, in the future, we would live in a golden age when there would be no more voyages by sea. Even though there are now faster means of transportation, maritime traffic has not decreased: 95 percent of the global transportation of material now takes place by sea. The sea, this shapeless, unmarked medium, a universe of danger and conquest, is now the risk society, deregulated spaces of finance and consumption over which the old nation-state appears to be a power without authority.

We are facing a configuration of the world that looks like the archaic form of the societies of hunters and gatherers, who conceive of the world more in terms of itineraries, plunder, and pacts than as closed spaces and stable properties. There is nothing strange about the figure of the pirate reappearing in a world like this, and it is not surprising that it continues to represent an ambiguity between freedom and barbarity. The pirate ship is a multiracial and multireligious utopia that one can choose to join, the celebration of the right to leave against the obligation of identity. There are various recent studies regarding the pirate economy and its peculiarities (Lesson 2009). The Marxist historian Christopher Hill (1973) pointed out that many radicals viewed piracy as more honorable than the sugarcane culture based on slavery.

The pirate embodies the type of enemy who does not threaten a particular country as much as land nations in general, not a concrete sovereignty as much as the idea of sovereignty in general. This is a person who, according to Philip Gosse, is "in defiance of all organized respectability." A pirate is distinct from a corsair in that he obeys no land laws and receives support from no land government. Cicero talked about people who are situated beyond the obligations of the "*immensa societate humani generis*" ["immense society of the human species"] (Gosse 1989 [1932], 1.53).

Within the taxonomy of enmity, pirates occupy a special place given their character as enemies of anyone who passes by. A pirate is not an individual enemy but everyone's common enemy (*communis hostis omnium*) (Heller-Roazen 2009). For the Roman philosopher, being part of the human community implies belonging to a clearly delimited territory. This is not the case for pirates, which explains their unsettling dangerousness.

Piracy is the opposite of hegemony, not in the sense that it is able to compete with empires in the power arena, but because it contests the idea of sovereignty itself. Piracy meddles in the intervals that the cycles of sovereignty continue to open, in "the space without witnesses, in the moral void" (Sloterdijk 2005, 180). This absolute hostility leads to our current designation of genocides as "crimes against humanity" or terrorists as "unlawful combatants." Modern terrorism is reminiscent less of a traditional war between nations than of the piracy that stems from the weakening of modern conventions on territorial war (Chomsky 2002; Innerarity 2004). We find ourselves facing "brigands," in the sense in which Bodino used the term to refer to those who do not respect the rules of the game (which also has unintended consequences, since turning the enemy into a "brigand" or a "fugitive" has served as an excuse for a strong decline of justice, for weakening democracy and international law). The parallelism between ancient piracy and current international terrorism is based on the fact that both phenomena are situated on the fringes of the territorial picture.

For this reason, I do not believe it is overextending the metaphor to affirm that piracy represents a new form of being in a world that has become liquid. I am referring not only to global terrorism but to current forms of globalization that once again take the bird of prey as a model. We could think about the behavior of consumers, which is so similar to pillaging (as is revealed by the first day of sales at the largest retailers or by any form of consumption that implies damage to the environment). The success of financial products would be inexplicable if it were not for the fact that they promise such large profits that we are blinded to the risks these products entail. I am also thinking about biopiracy, a term that appeared at the beginning of the 1990s to denote the unrightful appropriation of genetic resources. In this case, scientific or medical institutions are denounced as pirates, not because they destroy property, but because they introduce it into places where it did not previously exist. There is a relationship between many current conflicts and the regulation of certain natural resources; this could be called "a political ecology of war." In short, the current increase in pillaging is explained by the weakness of nations when it comes to effectively controlling their territories and by the worsening of particularly intolerable inequalities.

The analogy also proves its worth if we examine the current ideological panorama, more liquid than territorial, with political strategies that are closer to piracy than to traditional action. The current ideological disillusionment is manifested in the fact that neither the left nor the right is particularly interested in taking part in habitual pathways to representation. Both conservative individualism and radical leftism see themselves as "antiestablishment movements," as "parapolitics." The pirate, in both their ideologies, represents the paradigm of the fight against the rigidity of the state or against the neoliberal order; for various and even contradictory motives, piracy is considered the most adequate strategy for the economic and cultural evolution of capitalism.

Some theorists appeal to a civil society and others to the multitude (Hardt and Negri 2000); these are both very liquid and not very political concepts. We are no longer in an age of the institutionalized right- and left-wing, but in the age of the Tea Party and social movements. The right prefers the market over the state and the left—rather than traditional forms of labor, social, institutional, or armed struggle—formulates substitute battles like exile, defection, or nomadization. As Deleuze and Guattari suggested, the nomad, more than the proletariat, is the resistor par excellence (1972). On the left, the most innovative strategies reflect the decline of revolutionary ideals. The most they can aspire to is "détournement," a satirical parody proposed by contemporary art, making use of a term coined by the Situationist International. It implies attempted sabotage, derailment, distortion, or subversion. It is a question, in accordance with Deleuze, of interruptions or microspheres of insurrection. Of course, there is nothing reminiscent of the old goal of seizing power; the most ambitious proposal is to benefit from the interstices or the zones unoccupied by the state. Naomi Klein (2000), one of the principal advocates of the antiglobalization movement, appeals to "cultural jamming" as a form of resistance; this interference transforms brand advertising without altering its codes of communication in order to question the values these brands transmit. It is easy to note the contradiction of this alterglobalization, since choosing piracy demonstrates precisely that we do not believe "another world is possible."

Pillage, which was a common form of appropriation in the ancient and classical world and which the modern state attempted to resolve with the establishment of codified forms of property, has currently assumed (in the world of finances and information) enormously complex manifestations. One of the most telling entities of contemporary piracy is the tax haven, these places without identity, without taxation or residency requirements. What is claimed there is the unusual right to abandon political spaces and avoid the taxes that are a symbol of territorial power. This is another strategy of depolitization, in its most harmful form. It is no coincidence that many of these "havens" are islands, and those who go there are no longer reprobates but the elite who abandon territorial states and their restrictions.

Cyberspace also provides a great number of maritime and pirate metaphors. Like the oceans and the air, cyberspace is a territory of navigation. The vocabulary of the web is very explicit in this regard. We navigate the web, and pirates attack, immobilize, sabotage, and take over servers, sometimes just for fun, other times for criminal or geostrategic motives. Other surfers move about there with the same libertarian logic with which financial experts invent products to escape possible regulation. Hackers sneak through flawed portals in the web and financiers look for offshore spaces in the same way pirates circulate between spaces of sovereignty. Like historic pirates, those who navigate the web live in an archipelago over which the powerless state does not hold a monopoly on legitimate violence.

The dream of freedom is what has turned the Internet into a political utopia that has delighted a generation. Many commentators have emphasized the similarities between certain countercultural ideals and simple liberal anarchism. It is a question of what some have called "the Californian ideology" (Barbrook and Cameron 2001) since its origin resides in the anti-authoritarianism of the 1970s and has given way to an ideological proximity between market libertarians and the online community, between neoliberal hyperreality and virtual hyperreality, between hippie anarchism and economic liberalism. This curious mixture of McLuhan and Hayek is something that is not simply explained by a common belief in technological determinism; it has even deeper roots.

Luc Boltanski and Ève Chiapello (1999) have demonstrated how, following the rebellious movements of 1968, the criticism of capitalism has taken two different routes: a "social" route that demands a modification in the relationship between dominant forces and an "artistic" route that attempts to liberate individuals with the goal of making them more authentic and creative. The Internet has afforded the movement a means of expansion for the autonomy of the individual, self-organization, and the rejection of collective limits. This anti-institutional dimension establishes many similarities with libertarian ideology. It has been frequently pointed out that the antiestablishment hippies of the 1970s, who were so committed to individual autonomy, did not find it difficult to get used to liberal policies and deregulation.

In this way, a new online territory of political struggle has been created, which is dominated by freedom of information and a lack of trust in the face of authority and centralization. Free software advocates champion the dissolution of digital borders and defend the free distribution of products. They consider profits illegitimate because demand is connected not to the intrinsic superiority of a product but to the fact that it was there first, which frequently comes about by chance. On the other hand, it also seems excessive because those whose products are in demand attempt to make it irreversible by imposing, for example, artificial shortages and making duplication illegal or impossible. In order to combat the control of demand, the new pirates of cyberspace defend the right to produce knockoffs, which is criticized in the name of brand protection. These forms of piracy do not try to invert capitalism but to create spaces protected from general commercialization.

CAPITALISM WITHOUT PROPERTY

The lack of structure in the world today depends, to a large extent, on a series of changes that cannot be understood or regulated with the instruments that we have. The world is presented to us as a common reality, without an owner, in which it is difficult to establish responsibilities or allocate powers. This lack of organization corresponds with a profound transformation in the concept of property; one could even talk about its liquidation into a "capitalism without property."

We could explain this idea with a procedure that is valid for any historical reality. When we want to understand the meaning of something that is coming to an end, it is best to consider the meaning it had when it began. If the current crisis has revealed a profound transformation in capitalism, it could be enlightening to try to understand what the constitution of capitalism meant as a general system of property and commerce.

Therefore, what the modern state did was privilege property and property owners. All legal regulations afford great importance to the protection of property and distrust situations without an owner. Three-fourths of the articles of the French Civil Code of 1784 referred to property as the center of relationships and conflicts in a society. There was nothing in the world that could not become someone's property and nobody who could reject all relationships with property. Anyone who lacks property, who is completely uninterested in the stable possession of goods, is a public danger; that person could be a speculator, a pirate, a suicide bomber, or simply someone who does not deserve credit. People who lack property are dangerous because they do not truly move within society. Someone who is simply poor, on the other hand, requires state protection, consumes, even if not very much, and claims social recognition; that person can be a citizen, act responsibly, be locatable. That is why modern political systems believe that civic liberty cannot be exercised without property, no matter how minimal it is. In the second article of the *Declaration of the Rights of Man and of the Citizen*, property is found among the fundamental rights, alongside liberty, security, and resistance to oppression. However, what happens when the functioning of capitalism can renounce the ethics of property because it is no longer needed? What happens when property (its connections and its obligations) is no longer required to provide the necessary impulses to the market? This is the question that is currently being raised and that requires a new type of governance.

A survey carried out in Russia (and that could well be extrapolated to other countries) produced the following fact: responding to a question about which right they considered most important, a great majority situated the right to public health care, to work, or to education much higher than the right to property. We could conclude that the majority of Russians do not want to be landowners. A person with no interest in property is not interested in the state as a guarantee of that property either, only in an administration that guarantees certain benefits; those who live without property, in other words, without a private sphere, are not concerned about the public sphere either.

Globalized capitalism does not need property and its civic virtues. It has entered into a state of autonomy or self-reflexivity in which it can remain in motion without the civility that characterized what Macpherson called "possessive individualism" (1964). This is revealed in the current relationship between work and property. Property is no longer connected to managerial creativity and to work, which is no longer necessary when truly valuable property today comes from the value of stocks. At the same time, the ideal kind of worker is the autonomous technician who is not always present in the workplace, who maintains informal cooperation, who is not included in the solidarities of traditional work related to the production of material goods or formal hierarchical organizations. In the service economy, the ancient morality of work seems rather superfluous.

The scope of this capitalism without property is best seen in the financialization of the economy and in the world of stocks. Stocks are the new version of property. Even though not all property has to do directly or indirectly with the possession of stocks, it is in the stock market where the value of property is ultimately decided. Global financial markets establish the type of expectations that determine the movements of capital through stocks.

Property, which has been the expression of earnings, in other words, of a past, and which is connected with the idea of patrimony and inheritance, currently fluidifies until becoming the mere expectation that establishes the oscillation of stocks. If property used to symbolize continuity, the will of transmission toward posterity and, therefore, of perpetuating one's own existence in some way, it now has to dispense with such pretensions and be willing to react continuously to the movements of the stock market. The fluidification of property through stocks corresponds to the transformation of property in expectation. Success consists in skillful adaptation, without generation or responsibility, especially the civil responsibilities of property. Shareholders try to increase the value of their stocks, but not with the intention of strengthening the value of their property as inheritable wealth.

Current shareholders generally do not know what they are participating in with their stocks or how the company of which they are coowners is run. They passively follow the suggestions established by the great investment firms. They are owners of their property in appearance only. At the same time, they are easy prey to panic reactions, booty from movements of capital that do not reflect the objective value of things as much as emotional oscillations.

If that is true, then we should question the economic function of owning stocks, in other words, of providing a sign of progress and growth in the turmoil of market forces. Even though stocks are necessary to legitimize the market, they increasingly function as *claqueurs* for the movement of capital and for the development of companies, which only a few people are able to interpret. The economic and social strength of stocks consists theoretically in placing owners at the center of capitalist activity and turning them into business people. But the truth is that this barely holds for the majority of small and medium stockholders. Stocks are nothing more than an expectation of an increase in value; they do not belong to the world of property, something their owner can identify as available.

A capitalism configured in this way apparently does not need a stable framework to maintain its permanent agitation. But one of the things the economic crisis has highlighted is that we need to find a functional equivalent for the tasks that used to be fulfilled by states when there was a capitalism of owners; otherwise the current capitalism without property will cause market failures that we cannot, as civilized societies, accept.

UNGOVERNED SPACES

Many of the things that are happening seem to indicate that we are living in an "offshore" world, in other words, a world with power literally "distanced from the coast," delocalized, a world where the relevant authorities do not report to anyone: they are irresponsible and beyond the reach of legitimate political authority. As Palan (2003) would say, a world of sovereign markets, virtual places, and nomad millionaires. We have the feeling that those who should govern do not govern and those who are running things have no legitimacy. I am, of course, referring to the terrorists and men of war, but also, for example, to computer pirates, rating agencies, and tax evaders, who constitute a type of alternative authority or condition us in an unjustified manner, in ungoverned spaces, or wherever political authority is weak or clumsy.

The most serious and general examples of ungoverned spaces are those we denounce with the term "failed states," referring to societies where the nominal governments are incapable of exercising effective sovereignty. These political failures already have a long history. Following decolonization, it was hoped that new sovereign territories would follow the "Western" path of developing a sovereign power, in other words, the capacity for controlling the use of force, imposing political decisions within a territory, and resisting attacks from the outside. However, this paradigm has never adequately described the reality of two-thirds of the planet, where what exists is quasi-states or areas of limited sovereignty. This imbalance between legal sovereignty and effective sovereignty led to the emergence of alternative structures of authority in those areas: feudal forms of power, insurgency, tribalisms, mafias, and the like. Moreover, one might maintain that the inclusion of those decolonized spaces in the global economy has complicated their ability to organize a true political authority and exercise effective control in internal affairs. The structures of authority favored by global capitalism often do not coincide with the structures of authority that are granted legal sovereignty in those territories. This was a concern that, in the 1990s, after the end of the Cold War, gave way to the fear that terrorism would find refuge in those "failed states."

The concern about spaces that are ungoverned in the strict sense arises from the premise that the sovereignty of territorial states is the one correct form of political organization capable of guaranteeing world order. But this approach is too narrow because it does not address the ungoverned spaces that exist in the international system and in other virtual environments, with transnational actors and diverse networks, inside organized states, on the periphery, or in the center of many cities. We tend to see the problem of dangerous spaces as something exterior, which is an error because even in spaces beneath legitimate state sovereignty, the territory is not uniformly controlled. It has become too normal to find the existence of areas where one best not enter, within some cities, or in rural areas controlled by insurgents.

What if the difficulty of governing were less extraordinary, more disturbingly normal? In the first place, the state should be understood not only as a territorial space but as a functional and regulatory space. From this point of view, state authority always fails when it does not provide the benefits that are demanded of it, when it only regulates poorly or insufficiently. The problem of ungovernability is broader if we think of it not only in the extreme cases of power vacuums or state failure, but also as a general characteristic of the world in which we live. There are some who maintain specifically that the virtual spaces of finance and information presume the end of sovereignty (Strange 1996). In any case, it is interesting to consider how statehood has been transformed at a time of weak sovereignty; there are ungoverned spaces where states have ceded sovereignty, voluntarily or involuntarily, reasonably or not, in all or in part, to other authorities. If we understand that ungoverned spaces are those in which the power of the state is absent, weak, or contested, then, in addition to referring to territories of tribal power or persistent insurgence, we should widen our perspective to include the domain of the Internet or markets where economic agents operate without sufficient public regulation.

The wave of neoliberal globalization led to the deregulation of commerce and of the financial markets, which contributed to a significant decrease in the states' ability to regulate the flow of goods, services, information, people, technologies, and environmental damages. The origin of the current global financial crisis is to be found in the financial instruments that were developed in the space of the deregulated markets and dramatically illustrates the relationship between globalization, uncertain sovereignty, spaces of economic irresponsibility (such as offshore banks, tax havens, and a particular jurisdiction of banking secrecy), and the creation of alternative authorities (most notably the rating agencies, whose independence and sense of responsibility have been placed increasingly into question). The global spread of neoliberalism has undermined states' ability and legitimacy to govern the financial markets and create the conditions for balanced economic prosperity.

"Offshore" evokes exotic places and distant islands, but the truth of the matter is that the majority of the financial transactions of this type take place in the great financial centers of New York, London, and Tokyo. "Offshore" does not refer to the geographic location of certain economic activities but to the legal status of a series of places that are expanding because of the abstract character of current finances. This does not minimize the scandal of having the Cayman Islands be the fifth largest financial center in the world. Nor does it make any sense that Luxemburg has more banks than Switzerland, a country in which there are more bankers than dentists, or that Liberia has more boats than any other country in the world, or that the inhabitants of the Netherlands Antilles spend an average of three months a year making international calls.

The other case of unsettling deregulation is the Internet. Of course it is not a completely ungoverned space, because there is at least an unofficial partnership between governments and the companies that run it. In spite of everything, cyberspace continues to be a dangerous place; it is a truly transnational construction, where demarcations and borders have minimal relevance. Regarding the global nature of the information flow, the regulations are national and incomplete. The Internet possesses its own epidemiology similar to the pandemics of physical spaces as well as some specific crimes that are especially difficult to fight. Even though states still play an important role in the control of digital spaces (as seen in the uprisings in northern Africa and China), it is clear that governance of the Internet will diminish the centrality of the nation-state in global politics.

The conclusion we can reach from all of this is that there are more ungoverned spaces than we imagine, but they are less ungoverned than we fear. Things that initially appear disorganized often have their own type of order. Many of the goods traditionally provided by the states are now administered by local or transnational actors.

The prescription of governing these spaces is often realized from a state-centric perspective, as if the state—in its traditional form—were the critical actor when it comes to providing governance and generating security. But in the world of the twenty-first century, state sovereignty has become uncertain, and the state is accompanied by many other actors, benign and malign, which sometimes compete and sometimes collaborate when it comes to providing governance and security through nonhierarchical, horizontal forms of organization.

The concern about the loss of both functional and regional sovereign authority stems from the erosion of the territorial state as exclusive arbiter. In many cases, this concern is exaggerated; in other cases, it is reasonable, but it comes in response to the traditional states' weakness when it comes to executing the monopoly to which they aspire in a new multicentric world with diverse spheres of authority (Rosenau 1990). Many of the ungoverned spaces and the alternative authorities they represent are here to stay, like it or not, and states should worry about how to manage, limit, and coexist with them in order to provide their people with proper security. On many occasions, localizing the authority of the states within a network that includes nongovernmental organizations and international agencies contributes to the creation of systems that provide better norms and greater security. It is a question not of forgetting nominal sovereignty but of developing it with a more nuanced comprehension of the structures of authority that act in each area and every subsystem of society. The markets and cyberspace will become increasingly ungovernable if our understanding of governing is limited to the system of control that operated within traditional states. We must once again govern the things that social change tends to deformat politically; the problem is that it must be done in a different way.

IN SEARCH OF LOST RESPONSIBILITY

Piracy is an indicator of a lack of regulation, whether because we find ourselves faced with new forms of property, common goods that are hard to identify, or innovations that present normative problems. What should we think, for example, about that war on patents on the bottom of the sea in order to register organisms that could be applied to medical or energy needs? The new piracy is especially due to the current profusion of public goods, their natural lack of definition. In fact, the modern age could be understood as an age in which action was faster than legislation, as has been the case since modernity and as is probably a characteristic of modernity in general. Those who are looters and delinquents in stable, standardized times look like pioneers, adventurers, heroes, or missionaries of civilization during historical moments of discovery and expansion.

We should also consider pandemics, security, the climate, knowledge, the Internet, or financial risks, whose liquidity responds to the fact that it is not always easy to know who is in charge, who is the competition, to whom things belong, who will take responsibility, who is the originator, and so on. All of that is supplemented by a characteristic effect of deterritorialization: the difficulty of distinguishing private and public, that which belongs to me and that which belongs to everyone, internal and external. One must specify, for example, the conditions of acceptability of income in a knowledge and information society, when and to what extent the benefit for the creators (in the artistic, financial, and pharmaceutical fields) is legitimate. A new equilibrium must be found between the security and the defense of private life, between the originator's rights and the diffusion of culture, between the requirements of research and the right to health. We need, in short, new regulations for a world in which knowledge is scattered, from available information, from places within reach and instantaneous communication, a world of interdependencies and connections.

It would be worth interpreting the current attempt to regulate these new spaces as an attempt to reterritorialize the world and combat its excessive liquidity. It is the logic that moves the determination to control financial fluctuations and eliminate tax havens, which are no longer on the periphery but at the heart of the new global world. These lawless islands turn the relationship between land and sea on its head: solid land is now found on the periphery of a liquid world, states on the periphery of the financial world. It is as if we lived in a world in which the sea had assumed power over solid land. That is why the current battle against tax havens can be understood as the revenge of terrestrial powers against those derived from the new deterritorialized power.

Let us think, for example, about the idea of "traceability" that is presented as an ecological demand for consumer products, which is nothing but the attempt to go back up the chain of transactions to assign responsibility. What commonalities are found between the fact that a pirate had an unidentifiable past and no identifying attachment to any known state and uncertainties raised by many of the current food industry's products or the concerns certain consumer products raise when we presume their production comes from labor abuses? In both cases, it is the lack of past that produces fear. The idea of traceability is to depiratize the food chain and our consumption in general, regaining a confidence that can only be achieved by identifying its origin and historic evolution, replacing an ambiguity that conceals its liquid condition with a recognizable terrestrial itinerary.

But the problems are as vast as the confusion produced by a reality of such dense interdependencies. How are we to make war against the pirates in a liquid world in which there is not, strictly speaking, a battlefield? The repression of piracy in the eighteenth century provides a model that, give or take some obvious differences, can focus our battle against global crimes. The Alien Tort Statute, which the Americans used to try to eliminate pirates in 1789, gives us some clues about governance and global justice:

open debates, broader consensus, unification of criteria and laws. The fight against piracy could only be truly effective when it was thought of as an area of "universal jurisdiction," in other words, surpassing national jurisdiction.

The current ambivalence of deterritorialized realities reveals a problem for which we still have no adequate management framework. On the one hand, the fact that rights are valid regardless of the territory in which one finds oneself is progress. This is established, for example, in the United Nations Working Group on Arbitrary Detention: if a state exercises control over particular subjects, no matter the territory in which they are found, that state retains responsibility under international law. But there are perverse forms of deterritorialization such as Guantanamo, a whole series of no-man's-lands where it is established that the limits of territory are not necessarily coextensive with the limits of the law.

Current demands to move toward universal jurisdiction have their legal roots in the ancient right of anyone to pursue and penalize maritime looters. If we pay attention, many of humanity's biggest problems nowadays require going beyond territorial limits and finding "oceanic" solutions. For example, the demand for a revision and amplification of the criteria for access to citizenship in emigration matters, which would mean separating citizenship from the state or denationalizing rights. There is no other solution except overcoming the principal of territoriality of rights in consonance with the deterritorialized nature of the demands we should confront, making the law, in a manner of speaking, more "maritime" and less "continental," making it isomorphic with its object. The return of the pirates in the global age reveals that the sign of the times is the return of the seas and the progressive irrelevance of the land.

2

HUMANITY THREATENED

As Ulrich Beck says, unlike other previous civilizations, we cannot attribute everything that threatens us to external causes; societies are in conflict with themselves, with the production of that which they do not desire. Explaining this characteristic contrasts with our common sense, which tends to establish net causalities, distinguishes subjects from objects, thinks in terms of hierarchy, and explains the idea of defense in terms of spatial protection. To identify and understand the nature of threats in a world that belongs to everyone and to no one, we have no choice but to make a "metaphorological" effort. I am going to suggest three metaphors to correct our habitual way of thinking about these matters. I will begin with the idea that the world can be better explained according to the properties of gases, rather than liquids; secondly, I analyze the properties and effects of the excessive exposure in which we find ourselves during times of interdependency; and finally, I maintain that our world lacks outlying areas, in the sense that nothing, in fact, remains outside, peripheral, or completely isolated, and as a normative principle, we must not consider anything absolutely exterior. Between gaseous conditions, contagious realities, and spaces without closure, our understanding of the world in which we live is at stake, an understanding that is necessary if we are to be able to create something reasonable out of this world.

A GASEOUS WORLD

Metaphors can be dangerous toys, and that is why when people launch metaphors into the world, the metaphors simultaneously illuminate certain aspects of reality and verify their own limitations. In the same way that there is never light without shadows, there are no brilliant metaphors that do not occasionally blind us, preventing us from perceiving some aspects of reality that they wanted to clarify. That is what happened to the image of a society that had become "liquid," as the sociologist Zygmunt Bauman characterized the current world, a world of fluidity that contrasted with the rigidity of the nation-states and the traditional frameworks of government. According to this imagery, the geography establishing traditional geopolitics is modified and the central question revolves less around controlling geographic space and more around controlling liquid fluidity.

Nevertheless, no matter how seductive the metaphor of liquidity, it does not, in my opinion, adequately describe the entire reality of current social processes; this is why the regulatory attempts of national and international organizations fail, as has been repeatedly confirmed, when it comes to controlling immigration, capital flight, and the governance of climate change, to mention only a few telling examples. We are hitting the limits of what has been called "hydraulic Keynesianism." The metaphor of liquidity—given the homogeneous character of liquid elements—is not able to account for the global dimension of media turbulences—the buzz—that is created around events. This turbulence is initially explosive but quickly goes flat. Nor does the idea of liquidity sufficiently illustrate the phenomenon of financial bubbles, economic volatility, and speculation. When it comes to choosing an image that speaks for itself, Sloterdijk's bubbles (1998) have more explanatory strength to help us understand a world comprising phenomena that are more atmospheric than material, a world made up of hoaxes, rumors, haziness, risks, panic, speculation, and trust.

Explanatory limitations tend to be accompanied by strategic failures; inadequate theories are translated into ineffective actions. We have known for a while now that the control of the channels through which materials are exchanged does not guarantee the control of content. Even though Russia, for example, controls a significant segment of the global gas and petroleum market, its role in setting final prices in the markets of New York and London is minimal. Countries or actors that exercise no physical control over "liquid" channels of transfer have considerable influence in the setting of those prices. There is a growing disconnect between the fluidity of commerce, the fluidity of capital, and currency exchange. The weak relationship between currency exchange and the products on which it is based, the spectacular growth of options and futures markets, and economic speculation are all phenomena that have more in common with atmospheric unreality than with liquid elasticity. It is also true that there is an increasing divide between the intrinsic value of the underlying "liquid" that is circulating through tubes (gas, financial flows, information, and the like) and the use value for end users, a value that can "contract" or "explode" based on speculative oscillations.

The control of channels is not always crowned by success. This is especially evident when we try to place barriers on immigration by considering it a question of fluidity and channels, as if we had forgotten that this is an issue that depends more on general economic conditions. People do not emigrate because there are conduits between one country and another but because there are inequalities that the movement of workers tends to balance out, in the same way as the atmospheric pressures of air balance out. That is why strict border controls barely modify the final result of migratory fluidity; it is not slowed by any barrier but by decreased economic opportunities.

More than a liquid world, the process of globalization has led to a "gaseous world." This metaphor responds better to the reality of current financial markets and the mass media world since both are characterized, like volumes that contract and expand in the gaseous state, by cycles of expansion and contraction, growth and recession, a changeable volume. A gaseous world responds better to immaterial, vaporous, and volatile exchanges. These exchanges are very distant from the solid realities that characterized what we nostalgically call the real economy and are more complex than the movement of liquid fluidity. This image is also very appropriate for describing the increasingly uncontrollable nature of certain social processes, the fact that the whole world of finance, the media, and communications is based more on "gaseous" information than on fact checking.

In the new context of this gaseous world, the ability of international states or organisms to organize processes is as desirable as it is difficult. The proposed metaphor can help us understand the reasons behind this complexity. It is more difficult to control gaseous emissions than the circulation of a liquid. The great political problem of the contemporary world is how to organize things that are unstable. To do that, it is not enough to control the containers and channels of transmission, since an increasingly large number of exchanges are realized beyond traditional pathways and their use value depends increasingly on the particular conditions imposed by the end user.

Any attempt at regulation should focus on acting on the conditions and contexts that provoke the expansion or contraction of these speculative gaseous phenomena. The fundamental task for politics is to create a market environment whose essential parameters can be governed in some way. The classic and rigid act of channeling should be substituted by a flexible configuration that works at a distance, comparable to a magnetic field with electrical particles, in order to define the limits within which movements are free and not controlled. This flexibility would allow us to bring individual freedoms in line with the regulations that seem necessary so that free movement does not destroy the conditions of possibility, the system inside which they can act without provoking catastrophic situations.

Under these conditions, the effect of attraction is as mechanical as it is functional: the fluctuation that moves from one place to another is as banal as the winds that operate between two fields that have different pressures.

UNIVERSAL EXPOSURE

Humanity's principal concerns today are not concrete evils as much as indeterminate threats. We are not concerned about visible dangers but about vague risks that could spread anywhere, at the most unexpected time, and against which there is not sufficient protection. Of course, there are concrete dangers we can identify, but what most concerns us, for example, about terrorism is its unpredictable nature. What is most worrisome about the current economy is its volatility, in other words, the weakness of our instruments to protect us from financial instability. In general, much of our discomfort comes from how exposed we are to threats we can only partially control. Our ancestors lived in a more dangerous but less risky environment; the poverty in which they lived would certainly be intolerable for us today, but we are exposed to risks with which they were unfamiliar. If it is hard for us to understand the nature of these risks, they would have found them literally inconceivable.

Let us consider everything that has to do with the effects of climate change, the risks of nuclear energy, terrorist threats (so qualitatively different from the dangers of conventional warfare), the fallout of political instability, the financial repercussions of economic crises, the epidemics that need only the mobility of people and foodstuffs to arise, the consequences—unknown until recently—of the financialization of the economy, the spreading of rumors, distrust, and panic, which is as swift and uncontrollable as the speed of information, and so on. With all these phenomena, we experience the most worrisome part of the general interdependence that characterizes the globalized world: contagion, chains of events, pollution, turbulence, toxicity, instability, shared fragility, universal effects, overexposure. We could talk about the epidemic character of contemporary society (Lemarchand 2003; Neyrat 2004). At the heart of our discomfort, there is a "panicked fear of fluctuations that would flood the codes," which Deleuze and Guattari referred to some years ago and which the passing of time has done nothing but increase (1972, 164).

What is the cause of this feeling of excessive exposure and our resulting discomfort? We owe it to the reality of our mutual dependence, something that has in fact provided us many benefits. Talking about interdependence is a way of referring to the fact that we are exposed in an unprecedented fashion and do not have sufficient protection. Interdependence signifies mutual dependence, a shared lack of protection. We live in a world where "all things hang together," or, to say it in the language of Leibniz, "all things conspire." Nothing is completely isolated, and "foreign affairs" no longer exist; everything has become domestic. Other people's problems are now our own, and we cannot view them with indifference or wait for them to necessarily turn to our own advantage. This is the context of our unusual vulnerability. The things that used to protect us (distance, state intervention, foresight into the future, classic defensive procedures) have become weakened for various reasons and can now barely afford us sufficient protection.

We could affirm without exaggeration that there are no longer large distinctions between outside and inside, between nature and human, between that which is ours and that which is someone else's. Or to express it in a more unobjectionable manner, these distinctions are no longer clear and noncontroversial. "The Great Divides" that were until recently organized by our living spaces should, according to Latour, be seen as intertwined dimensions, affording some novel ways of thinking (Latour 1999). This is what Ulrich Beck called "boundarylessness": there is no way to expel to the exterior the undesirable consequences of our actions, which will end up affecting us like a boomerang. We could call this the fundamental self-influencing of the modern world.

Perhaps we have not deduced all the geopolitical consequences that stem from these new realities and make us so dependent on one another. In such an intermingled world, not even the most powerful among us is sufficiently protected: hegemony collides with the fact that, even though those who are less powerful have never been unimportant, fragmentation and empowerment now create situations that are off-balance and asymmetrical and not always favorable to the will of the powerful. The weak, when it is clear they are not going to win, can damage those who are strong and even make them lose in the end. While each individual state created its own laws under the Westphalian model, in a world of interdependencies, the strongest is continuously held hostage to the weakest, regarding its security, its health, its economic stability, or the protection of "its" environment. Everyone is exposed to the effects of the disorder and turbulences that develop on the periphery.

When borders are blurred in such a way that it is not easy to determine what belongs to us or to someone else, when phenomena circulate and expand very quickly, when there is no action without a response, it is logical that the problem of threats and protections is considered with greater urgency, although sometimes in an unreasonable manner. In the absence of global protections and in view of the weak security that states afford, individuals search for immunological microspheres like walls, cars, the stigmatizing of the Other, protectionisms, segregation, and so on. That is why there is an entire paranoid politics that pursues borders, insists on recuperating the old distinction between the outside and the inside and the separatist insularities that try to achieve total immunity.

The problem is that certain defense mechanisms are dangerous, and they end up being potentially self-destructive when attempting to be protective. Separatist bubbles run the risk of transforming themselves into redundant protections that provoke disasters that are similar to the ones they are trying to ward off. Let us think about dangerous combinations of medications, preventive wars that are lost, walls that, rather than protecting us against evil, isolate us from good and exacerbate hatred toward the Other. Perhaps what best illustrates this paradoxical connection between overexposure and overimmunization, the logic of harmful protections, is the image of drivers who straddle two contradictory automotive realities: that double, ambivalent condition between maximum exposure and the sense of maximum immunity.

But how do we wake up from the dream of immunity? How do we protect ourselves without self-destructing? Among the risks of "immunopolitics" (Sloterdijk 1998; Esposito 2002) is the destruction of the community, of sharing, because of the asymmetry of protections. The worst inequalities are expressed in the social dualization between those who are immune and those who are fully exposed. The community destroys itself when there is no reciprocity or interaction because a community is a particular community of risks. In a society that is excessively and unequally protected, we do not have community but distinct spheres of self-protection that allow us to "place the other at a distance," thus configuring a species of "intangible bodies" (Brossat 2003, 15).

But there is also a question of principle that reveals the paradoxes of all immunity. Anyone who wants to be protected must start by limiting the scope and extent of their security measures, if they do not want to destroy themselves in case the security measures go beyond the destruction of supposedly pathogenic elements. They must, therefore, "protect themselves against their own protection, their own police, their own power of rejection, their own isolation, in other words, against their own immunity" (Derrida 2001, 67). Total immunity, the success of protections, would, according to Derrida, be absolute evil, equivalent to self-destruction. Absolute evil is the failure of absolute protection, or in other words, its complete success.

This overexposed situation is largely unfamiliar, which is why it raises numerous interrogatives for which we do not have suitable answers. What can protections be like in this type of world?

We must, first of all, overcome the temptation to produce spheres of impenetrable security. A perfect enclosure is impossible and the dream of that impossibility demands considerable energy. We should learn from the human organism, which boasts systems of protection that are very sophisticated but less rigid than we generally suppose or would, in principle, desire. But the fact is that we owe our extraordinary survival to the flexibility of our defenses.

If ecology has afforded us the model of systematic thinking, we could consider a global ecopolitics that kept some of its properties in mind. In the first place, it is important to realize that a human being has ten times more symbiotic micro-organisms than cells of his or her own. It is even possible to say that the organism is more exogenous than endogenous. There is a true symbiosis in the case of intestinal bacteria, which are crucial for digestion. We also find that some of the micro-organisms that we tolerate play a role in our immune system. It makes no sense, therefore, to consider bacteria as dangerous externalities and the immunity of the organism as a fight to the death against everything that is different from it. On the contrary, considering immunity from the point of view of tolerance, interactions, and habitual internalization means accepting that the organism is not separated from its surroundings or absolutely protected in the face of external influences. That which we could call barriers—like skin or mucous membranes—are places that are more given to exchange than to isolation. The organism is not only capable of interiorizing external beings, but this internalization is needed for its preservation, for its normal functioning, its immunity.

Of course life is not possible without protection. If separatist bubbles are dangerous, pure exposure to everything that pops up is unthinkable. But protections are effective when they allow for a certain type of relationship and when they are integrated into processes of building common ground.

It is not strange that a vulnerable, contagious globality inevitably triggers strategies of prevention and protection, which are not always effective or reasonable and often turn into hysterical reactions, unfounded fears, and disproportionate responses. Many of our current defense strategies—whose icon par excellence could be the construction of barriers—are either literally ineffectual or awaken feelings of fear and xenophobia that end up doing more damage to us as a society than that from which we wanted to protect ourselves could do. In the age of global warming, intelligent bombs, digital attacks, and global epidemics, our societies should be protected with strategies that are more complex and subtle. We cannot continue with procedures that seem to ignore the environment of interdependence and the common exposure to these global risks.

We must learn a new grammar of power in a world that is made up of more shared opportunities and shared threats than self-interest. Self-interest has not disappeared, of course, but it is untenable outside of the framework of the communal process in which we are all implicated. While the ancient power struggle promoted the protection of that which belongs to us and indifference toward that which belongs to others, overexposure forces us to mutualize risks, developing cooperative procedures, sharing information and strategies. We must deepen the debate that points toward global governance, the horizon that humanity should pursue today with the greatest of energies. It sounds difficult, but it is certainly not pessimistic: governing global risks is humanity's great imperative if we do not want the thesis of the end of history to be verified, not as an apotheosis of the placid victory of liberal democracy, but as our worst collective failure.

A WORLD WITHOUT OUTLYING AREAS

We may owe the first formulation of the idea of globalization to Kant when he warned that, given the spherical surface of the earth, we all end up encountering one another: human beings cannot be dispersed indefinitely, so we have no choice but to tolerate other people's company. If the world were shaped differently, dispersion, the protection of some against others, definitive isolation, or exclusion would be possible (Kant 1968a, 6, 358). The fact that everything is connected to everything invites us to consider the world as a unified system (which does not exclude the possibility of asymmetries and malfunctions). Initiatives generate resistance in this system; the separation between that which is inside and that which is outside becomes problematic, and we are all exposed to the same difficult conditions.

In all likelihood, we owe this consciousness of sharing a common fate to the presence of risks that threaten us equally and relativize the distinction between individual and common concerns. In the same way that these undesired risks do not respect delimitations or areas of sovereignty, the shared world is constituted as a suppression of rigid differences between what is ours and what is someone else's. The contrast between self-interest and public interest is increasingly useless, just as the contrast between here and there is disappearing. We can explain this odd juxtaposition through the metaphor of a world that has lost its outlying areas, its outer edge, outskirts, suburbs (Innerarity 2004, 119–127).

A thing can be considered global when it leaves nothing outside of itself, when it contains everything, connecting and integrating so that nothing remains loose, isolated, independent, lost or protected, saved or condemned, outside. The "rest of the world" is a fiction or a way of speaking when there is nothing that does not in some way belong to our common world. In a world without outlying areas, close or immediate is no longer the only dimension available, and the horizon of references is notably expanded. The tyranny of closeness is relaxed, and other considerations come into play. This could be formulated with Martin Shaw's precise expression: "there are no others" (1996). For Beck, globalization also means the experience of a civilizing self-threat that suppresses the mere plural juxtaposition of peoples and cultures and introduces them into a unified space, into a cosmopolitan unity of destiny (2002, 37–38). Along similar lines, David Held speaks of communities "that share a common destiny" to indicate that the globalization of risks creates an involuntary community, an unintended coalition, which means that no one is left outside of this common fate (2000, 400; see also Albrow 1996; Robertson 1992).

The suppression of the outer edge implies the end of two habitual operations that are like two sides of the same coin: assuring one's own immunity and pushing what is undesirable toward the edges. When outlying areas existed, there were a series of operations that allowed us to make use of those marginalized spaces. It was possible to flee, wash one's hands, ignore, protect. There was some logic to the exclusivity of one's own possessions, one's own practice, the good of the country. The disappearance of outlying areas, to the extent that it eliminates the distinction between interior and exterior, results in the loss of a free trade zone from which other people's failures can be observed with equanimity. It signifies, therefore, the end of any guarantee of immunity. It makes difficult and precarious the perimeterization that, whether spatial or temporal, would allow us to protect ourselves from certain problems.

On the other hand, when we had outlying areas, almost everything could be resolved with the simple operation of externalizing problems, pushing them to the edge, outside of our field of vision, to a distant place or another time. An outlying area is specifically a place where we can simply discard unresolved problems, waste products, a garbage dump. The modern theory of the sovereign nation-state was expressly configured to move the problem of chaos to the outside: Hobbes assured internal order with a concept of sovereignty that meant "exporting" anarchy to the outside, thus configuring a competitive international system.

Perhaps the most beneficial side of the civilizing process and the advancement in the construction of spaces for the common world can be formulated through this concept of suppressing outlying areas. Without needing anyone to sanction it expressly, it is increasingly difficult to hand responsibility off to other people, to distant regions, to future generations, to other social sectors. Globalization presumes the impossibility of expelling the Other to a location beyond our reach. Our greatest progress takes the form of obliging interiorization and forbidding externalization.

This is because a world without outlying areas is a world that has been configured systemically, in other words, from the consciousness that all initiatives contain a principle of resistance, there is no action without reaction, plan without side effects, decision without protest, sovereign who is not observed. No one can be completely passive or merely a receptor. Everyone who acts in a global, interdependent world must confront the consequences of what they are doing in an especially intense manner. It is the time for cooperation, but also for reciprocal impediments. When we ask someone for cooperation, we are at least recognizing that person's capacity to obstruct, which is the most elemental form of sovereignty.

We find the breakdown of the rigid dichotomy between interior and exterior on the basis of this rebalancing of the world. We must not forget that the collective goods for which the nation-states took responsibility have been defined as those from whose use and enjoyment "insiders" cannot be excluded while procedures existed to authorize the exclusion of "outsiders" (Olson 1971). Complex systems, on the other hand, are characterized by "overlapping memberships" and "cross-cutting affiliations." Many of the debates that have recently arisen would not have been considered when the traditional limits between the inside and the outside were fully operable. After developing an entirely new legitimation of military interventions or humanitarian aid, for example, after the intense discussion surrounding transnational regulations or universal jurisdiction, there is even talk of a "right to monetary interference" that, considering the reality of globalization, could regulate the international credit market.

All these circumstances presume, at the same time, an extraordinary increase in what must be considered public space and a previously unknown difficulty with configuring common spaces for which we do not currently have adequate instruments. This complication stems from the most radical transformation realized by a world that tends to eliminate its outlying areas, namely, the difficulty of defining limits and establishing any strategy based on them (be it organizational, military, political, economic). In the best-case scenario, when it is possible to fix the limits, we must also know that any construction of limits is variable, plural, contextual and that the limits must be defined and justified over and over again, according to the matter under consideration. The immediate consequence is that the interior and exterior of any activity are continually confused. While we most likely have not yet drawn all the conclusions that derive from this fact, we must now accept as indisputable truth that no important problem can be resolved locally and that, strictly speaking, internal politics and external affairs no longer exist. Everything has become internal politics. The number of problems that governments can only resolve cooperatively is increasing, at the same time as the authority of transnational organizations is strengthened and the principle of nonintervention in other nations' affairs loses legitimacy. The limits between internal and external politics have become extremely vague; "external" factors like global risks, international standards, or transnational agents have become "internal variables." Our way of conceiving and implementing political decisions will not be up to the challenges we are facing if the distinctions between "inside" and "outside," between "us" and "them," are not placed into question as concepts that do not help govern within geographically unlimited areas (Grande and Risse 2000, 251).

The world is already a collection of intertwined destinies, of spaces that overlap, an involuntary implication that leads to unusual communities and spaces in which a common destiny is at stake. Our destinies are implicated to the extent that we share a common fate. Globalization is a mixture of shared goods and opportunities; it empowers us all and makes us particularly vulnerable. It is something that becomes especially painful with common problems that, like catastrophes, know no limits and stop at no barrier. Another of our most startling paradoxes is evidenced here: we have acquired a greater sense of the unity of the human race in the face of evil than in view of the good, in other words, before global problems like peace and war, security, the environment, pollution, climate change, food risks, financial crises, migrations, or the effects of technological and scientific innovations. That is why one could speak of risk as a potentially unifying factor (Habermas 1996) or of the productive and mobilizing force of dangers (Jonas 1979). The consequences of humanity's civilizing experiment place us within a framework of dependencies that forces us to take the interests of others into account in order to protect our own interests. Although the solution to these problems is still controversial, the conflicts themselves have an integrating function, to the extent that they reveal the need to find common or negotiated solutions.

The starting point for constructing a world of common goods consists in understanding the implications of diverse spaces in a destiny that tends to be unified or, at least, getting rid of any limitation of areas and subjects, as national belief systems have always preferred. One cannot understand the current world situation without taking into account the intrinsically polemical nature of the question, who are we? Globalization is a process that makes the determination of one's own identity broader and more complex, more permeable and interconnected with other collective destinies. In the era of globalization—in the era of interlaced destinies, of side effects that affect all of us—we again find validity in Dewey's idea (1988 [1927]; see also Beck and Grande 2004, 63) that politics creates its own public spaces according to what is in play at any given time: political controversies do not arise in the places where decisions are made as much as in the diverse contexts where the dramatic consequences of those decisions are perceived. Be that as it may, a globalized government would then have to become something like a regime of side effects, whose scope of action does not coincide with national limits.

The political arena then becomes everything that is perceived as a bothersome consequence of society's decisions.

From this point of view, we can understand that the current economic crisis does a very good job of exemplifying the nature of globalization and the idea that we are in a world without surroundings. First off, it can be claimed without exaggeration that it is probably the first truly global economic crisis, a crisis where globality aggravated the crisis. Normally economic and financial relations tend to play a moderating role in national crises. International movements of capital and variations in exchange rates allow us to minimize the initial impact by diverting part of it toward the "rest of the world." But in the case of a global crisis, on the other hand, there is no "rest of the world" that can perform this moderating function, and the crisis cannot help but deploy its internal logic until the end. In fact, it has already been observed that synchronized international crises are stronger and more economically costly than other crises. This is even truer for global crises, to the extent that we are not equipped with institutions capable of managing this globalization and its risks.

On the other hand, the crisis has revealed the inconvenience of distinguishing what is inside and outside, failing to note their interaction. In the financial arena, for example, banking regulation has been revealed to be ineffective given its microprudential nature. In other words, it takes into account the risk related to the insolvency of a particular banking entity, but not the insolvency of the banking system in general (which it tends, on the other hand, to provoke). The regulations have prompted a very harmful distinction between the balance of the banks and the lack of balance of products. The things that are "out of balance" have acted as if they were "outside," and that, as we have seen, no longer functions. The banking system can be affected as much by an upsurge of internal risks to its balance as by an upsurge of external risks to its balance, once this upsurge reaches a certain breadth and acquires a systemic dimension. The search for a lesser risk at any cost, whether by overcoming the risks to the bank balance (through securitization and derivatives) or through ever-higher capital demands, runs the risk of pernicious side effects.

If this is the nature of the crisis, then the need to provide a systemic and cooperative response is clear. Financial imbalances have largely been due to regulators' inability to exchange information, to the fact that—in the best of circumstances—states have merely juxtaposed national politics, offering no global response to the crisis. But the failure of cooperation that was the true cause of the crisis of 1929 reveals that we are now living in a new age where states are no longer in any position to pursue their interests without taking the interests of others into account in some way. States must abandon that stage in which they have had great difficulties in managing interdependencies and transnational externalities as soon as possible. The horizon of financial governance registers increasingly as an unavoidable reference, once we realize that the interstate framework is inadequate, incapable of dealing effectively with a global crisis and, more generally, of preventing global economic and financial instability.

In the end, this all leads us to a reconsideration of legitimacy as inclusion. Metaphors of garbage and immunity point toward the same demand for inclusion, the fight against asymmetries and their increasing discomfort: the spatial asymmetry between the territorial nature of the states and the global nature of many of our problems; the temporal asymmetry that advises us to adopt an intergenerational perspective when it comes to adopting certain decisions (all the decisions that have to do with sustainability) beyond the fixation on the current legislature; cognitive asymmetry that stems from the complexity of political questions and requires realizing new equilibriums between expert knowledge and the demands for participation. It is not strange that there is an intensification in the demand for a reduction in the distance between decision makers and shareholders, between those who decide and those who are affected by those decisions, in such a way that symmetry is restored between those who act and those who suffer and the connection between political geography and economic geography is reestablished.

The processes aimed at politicizing globalization have the same legitimacy as the processes aimed at political decentralization and similar goals: in all such cases, there is an attempt to allow for the possibility of including those who find themselves significantly affected by a decision. All democratizing impulses have come from the scandal of having binding decisions that not everyone has accepted. This is also the case with globalization, even if we know that the procedures for democratizing globalization will need to be more complex than the procedures that served for the configuration of nation-states. In this respect, David Held (2005, 252) formulated a criterion for drawing proper boundaries that required calculating the range of people whose life expectancies are significantly affected by a particular decision. It is safe to assume that we will have more intense discussions in the future about the appropriate jurisdiction for handling public goods, for avoiding unacceptable power imbalances during the decision-making process, or for thinking that market forces are capable of resolving these questions.

PART II

THE UNFULFILLED PROMISE OF PROTECTION

3

GLOBAL FEAR

When you want to understand a society, it is more useful to examine its fears than its desires. We could say: Tell me whom you are afraid of and I will tell you who you are. We can now register a fear with new characteristics in the fear taxonomy, and we could call it global fear, in other words, fear of the consequences of the process of globalization. It is a question of risks that have to be governed and from which we have the right to be protected. At the same time, unreasonable reactions to some of the concerns raised by this process express the pathologies of a global "I" that reacts with authoritarianism in order to compensate for its own impotence. This subject is both insecure and tyrannical, apathetic and voracious. This ambiguity closely matches the properties of Bauman's "liquid fear": an indistinct and vague fear that begins with the perception of the loss of control over events. This is how we can understand the siege sensation felt by a large part of the Western world, a world that is enjoying a situation of objective security unlike any other previous time in the history of humanity.

THE RATIONALITY OF FEAR

Being frightened is an essential part of the human condition. We all feel frightened, and it does not seem we will stop feeling that way, although the motives for fear can be very diverse throughout the world and throughout time. Every moment in history is differentiated from others by the particular forms of fear it knows, or, rather, by the name or particular meaning given to the anxieties that have always accompanied social life. Jean Delumeau (1989), Corey Robin (2004), and Joanna Bourke (2005) have written remarkable books that explain how the perception of fear has changed over the course of time. What remains to be explained is the nature of the global fear that is currently in place at a time when humanity seems to have secured its victory in the face of the randomness of nature and the brutality of social conflict. Texts by Bauman (2006) and Pulcini (2009) attempt to resolve this enigmatic paradox.

How is it possible that a secure society coincides in time with a civilization of fear, that we are more fearful when there are less objective motivations for fear? First of all, because in our society many fears are due precisely to the increase in security; the habit of security has made the perception of loss more acute. We live in a world in which we can lose more because we have so much, in contrast to a world where we could gain more because we had very little. A psychological explanation has to do with the aversion to loss: people consider a loss of status more undesirable than they consider a gain desirable. The displeasure of losing what we have is greater than the pleasure engendered when there is a possibility of improving what we have (Sunstein 2005, 41).

The paradox is also explained by means of the distinction between old dangers and current risks. In traditional societies there were large fears but they were rather foreseeable: shortages, hunger, illness, war. The improbable was situated in a background category of constant fear, which one could deal with in a way. In contrast, current sources of fear are more uncertain and indeterminate; we now see the world as more risk-filled than danger-filled. We cannot program risks in our society; we do not have a list of them. The element of improbability cannot be mastered, particularly in a cognitive manner. The current increase in fear is due not only to the fact that certain risks that threaten society have increased but to the fact that the conditions of uncertainty in which people spend their lives have increased. Our society is constantly exposed to the imponderable. The world has become more complex, and we have not managed to rise to the occasion of that complexity. For that reason, the space of the imaginary and its political use is enormously expanded: wars are fought, elections are won, and governments act in the imaginary realm.

To understand these paradigm changes, we need to take into account the distinct function that fear has had on the construction of modern political community or on the current fragility of globalized spaces. Fear is the passion that is at the heart of life in common. If we reread Hobbes, we will find documentation of this transition that we can now recall concisely. Human beings have a similar capacity for mutual destruction. The fear of death caused by other people leads individuals to the construction of a civil and political society that guarantees security. The goal of self-preservation is at the core of the creation of the modern state. Submission to the sovereign is the price one must pay to stop fearing our fellow human beings.

This is no longer the way it is in the global age. We continue to be afraid of many things, of course, but what has weakened is the productive metamorphosis of fear, its transformation into rational action that configures common institutions. Fear has become ineffective, unproductive, and desperate. The surges of fear that are appearing nowadays no longer contain the productive force that established the political institutions of modernity.

At the same time, we can see that the two main ways of liberating people from fear, through technological and through political intervention, have lost a good deal of their efficacy. Technology has become a multiplier of risk and uncertainty, while politics, in its classic state form, is incapable of confronting the challenges of globalization. In this context, how do we avoid succumbing once again to the "illiteracy of fear" that Musil addressed and that reveals our inability to experience fear in a reasonable manner?

In addition to being politically unproductive, global fear is characterized by arising from the uneasiness provoked by someone *different* rather the potential threat of someone *similar*. The Other, the foreigner, anyone who is distinct, comes to represent a disturbing difference. As in the global era, the outside/inside distinction does not work with Hobbesian clarity. It is no longer possible to banish the foreigner or enemy and thus secure one's own threatened identity. The Other, the foreigner, is now among us. We do not fear a symmetrical conflict—which presupposes equality—as much as assimilation or contamination. The Other who inspires fear is no longer someone similar (with a similarity that is hostile and whose dangerousness arises from the fact, according to a basic Hobbesian way of thinking, that he or she possesses the same destructive capacity as I do), but someone who is different, from an ethnic, religious, cultural, or ideological standpoint. Given that contemporary fear is not enflamed by those who are the same but by those who are different, this fear cannot be easily shifted so that the equality of threats will be transformed into an equality of rights.

This point also reveals the profoundly antimodern and unproductive nature of our current fears.

For the creation or maintenance of a democratic society, fear is not good or bad; everything depends on the use that is made of this elemental human passion. Our biggest current challenge is to give it a reasonable direction, for example, transforming it into a constructive force that allows us to know reality better and to strengthen democratic coexistence. We need to be in harmony with fear and manage the double-sided ambiguity that characterizes it: it can paralyze, but it can also organize strategies for defense and construction. Fear is not only paralyzing, but organizational. If well managed, it can offer us a solid cognitive dimension in the face of risk. This ability to recognize dangers and consider them in their just measure is what Hans Jonas (1984) called "the heuristics of fear," inviting us not to scorn this magnificent resource, which allows the imagination of the most terrible things to become a reasonable spur for action. In that way, the principal problem we have is not the "freedom from fear," to use Roosevelt's famous formulation, but the "freedom to fear," as Günther Anders (1956) suggested, the freedom to be afraid, which presupposes the capacity to feel sufficient fear if we want to free ourselves from the true dangers that threaten us.

Fear is not only an instrument of control for the elites but a fundamental and universal passion, whose first and indispensable function is to guarantee the self-preservation of individuals by keeping the memory of their vulnerability alive within them (Robin 2004). Among other things, politics serves to cultivate in society a proportional and reasonable fear. Of course there is an antidemocratic, populist "creation of fear," which stigmatizes in order to try to neutralize the democratizing potentialities of pluralism; fear can be skillfully stoked in order to offer itself as a savior or to induce lethargy in a society in such a way that it is more easily governable. But there is fear that can be a source of lucidity and liberation. The opportune dramatization of risks is an antidote against the simple-minded present that does not know how to do anything but continue muddling through (Beck 1997). In relation to many of the true threats we confront, reactivating fear can help us abandon our self-destructive passivity and recuperate the mobilizing force against disaster.

One of our principal tasks is precisely to rationalize global fear, a fear that is very logical given humanity's common exposure to the risk of self-destruction, the mutual interdependence that connects us to the destiny of those who are similar to us. Vulnerability, negated by subjects who saw themselves as sovereign and self-sufficient, can become the premise for the formation of a subject in relation, capable of taking responsibility for the other and the world (Pulcini 2009, 264). But what if the preservation of the world is the Copernican revolution of the global era? The ideal of caring for and conserving would lose its static and antiprogressive resonance to assume an emancipating significance. In that way, the task at hand could truly unsettle that predatory, parasitic, consumerist, viewing subject, who is now dying of fear.

GOVERNING GLOBAL RISKS

The British magazine *Economist* defines itself in this way: published since 1843 "to take part in a severe contest between intelligence, which presses forward, and an unworthy, timid ignorance obstructing our progress." This liberal declaration, with its epic touch, now has an anachronistic tone. Apart from a few heroic exceptions, we can say today that precaution has replaced planning itself and that our relationship with the future tends to focus on prevention.

For those who grew up with the fears of the 1970s and 1980s (growth and its limits, the nuclear threat, the ecological crisis, shortage of resources, and so on), the word "progress" sounds frivolous. Now, in the midst of the financial crisis, using the language of management, which exalts the culture of risk and the willingness to fail, seems like a provocation. In general, being a progressive today has nothing to do with progress, but rather with precaution toward science and technology. Therefore, it is not unusual to quote Benjamin's quip against Marx, saying that the revolution is the emergency handbrake of history. Currently, after the financial crises and the problems of climate change, the provocative nature of the idea of progress has only intensified.

The presumption of the danger inherent in technological and scientific innovations has progressively filled the ideological void that appeared after the collapse of the idea of the ingenuity of progress. Novelty and progress are presented under the aegis of risk. What began as skepticism of the vanguard has now become a commonplace. In the best of cases, we expect politics to be able to ward off the threats that may appear in the future. It is not surprising that the idea of sustainable development has aroused so much interest or that the principle of precaution has been formulated and applied with such intensity.

Considering the gravity of the risks we are confronting, fear is not entirely unfounded. There are those who disapprove of the excess of alerts and the aversion to risk, which is seen as a paranoia suffered in wealthy countries. Of course, hysteria is hardly a reasonable means of confronting risks, but that does not mean they do not exist. Risks continue to be a source of anxiety even when our way of confronting them may be exaggerated or ridiculous. What we need is a profound study of the limits of precaution.

Let us take a look at a recent example. The winter of 2009 and 2010 will probably go down in history as the Era of Alerts, among which we could mention swine flu and the prevention of certain potentially catastrophic weather events. I do not know whether this came from the guilty conscience of not having anticipated the economic crisis, but the fact of the matter is that governments outdid themselves in sounding alarms over possible contagions or storms, whose very names (for example, "explosive cyclogenesis" and "the perfect storm") were themselves colored by a note of warning. Governments preferred to give warning rather than face later accusations of not having foreseen the worst. This attitude seems very sensible, but it also entails some inconvenience, even when things do not go as poorly as we were made to fear. The fact is that not all risks can be given the same attention; every preventive action comes at a price, whether that cost is strictly financial or whether it is a result of the inevitable selectivity of prevention, where emphasizing one risk implies disregarding another. No one demands that anyone be held accountable for inducing panic, the costs of fear, the money wasted, or the attention diverted from other important matters. An excess of alerts is less serious than a shortage of them, but it is not an ideal solution either.

The lesson we should draw from excessive alerts is that programs meant to avoid all risks generate counterproductive effects. Attempting to completely eliminate fear through total prevention is absurd because fears are part of the human condition, our open character, and the corresponding indeterminacy of liberal democracies (Sunstein 2005). Preventions tend to imply some prohibition and should, in an open society, be established—with the greatest possible prevention. A generalized prohibition on innovation would be very risky. Where would society then get the innovations necessary to fight hunger, disease, poverty, or natural disasters? The relative irresponsibility of science is the foundation of its success, and no one currently holds a monopoly on the ability to distinguish bad risks from good innovations.

Prevention has its costs, and it is frequently the case that banishing one fear creates another. One recent example is found in the change the World Health Organization made in the definition of "pandemic." This change allows medicines and vaccines to be introduced in an emergency fashion, in other words, with less guarantees and greater risks. We could also mention the danger of spreading fear and its side effects or the perverse consequences of exaggerated and unnecessary laws. Prevention also has its risks, especially when it is redundant (Wildavsky 1988). All of this also must be considered within a temporal perspective: many models and methods that were previously recognized in good conscience as reliable advances now appear to be exercises in irresponsible frivolity.

I do not think it is going too far to state that in the future our principal discussions will revolve around the question of how we evaluate risks and what actions we recommend as a consequence. Political confrontation focuses on the probabilities of danger and the anticipation of risks. Politics is more of a competition focused on dangers than on opportunities. Political actors are similar in that they all focus equally on warning us about the imminence of certain dangers, offering to save us from disaster; they differ only in the risks they consider most dangerous: a loss of identity or the lack of social protection, risks related to a lack of safety or to possible abuses by those who are standing guard. But they hardly even try to imagine what would be *desirable* because of the fear of *possible* evils. The rivalry of threats seems to have replaced the rivalry between projects. Political agents wield less ideology than resources to sound the alarm.

These controversies are fueled by the fact that the perception of risk has a strong degree of subjectivity. Ulrich Beck (2006) ventured to say that this contrast could be extended to a planetary scale and generate a "war of risk religions." The fact that some cultures fear what is considered normal in others takes on new geopolitical significance. Now that countries like China or India are on the First World stage, we are confronted by risk cultures very different than those to which we are accustomed. Different risk cultures tend to find opportunity in every danger, the appearance of which is weighed in terms of likelihood. Risk taking that we previously considered normal is going to appear less and less normal.

This debate has intensified since the question of global risks has appeared on the political agenda. Climate change, new security threats, health and food risks, and financial crises immediately challenge our conception of these uncertain futures. How can we recognize possible risks? How should we act in relation to risks that are not verifiable facts but latent possibilities whose very identification is open to controversy? How do we remain cognizant of the improbable? Every uncertain future confronts us with dilemmas that are particularly difficult. What precautions are reasonable? How can we preempt the causal chains of disaster? What type of concerted action is appropriate for the global treatment of our problems? How can we manage our inevitable ignorance of future events? And so on.

First, we need to fully understand the nature of those risks if we want to properly manage the uncertainty they imply. Risks, particularly global risks, resist calculation according to scientific criteria, so faith in their existence or lack thereof becomes decisive. It makes no sense to contrast the "poorly informed opinions" people hold about presumed risks with the rational views experts hold on actual risks. All too often, expert rationalism, with its calculation of probability, is as full of errors as when alarmists exalt fear as the supreme bestower of knowledge. Populist alarmism is just as suspicious as technocratic frivolity.

We must agree about acceptable risks. Many decisions regarding risk are not a question of selecting between secure or risky alternatives, but require making a choice between alternatives that are always risky. As I just mentioned, all preventive measures imply risks, because of both what we do and what we fail to do. Fear is a sign, and signs should be neither ignored nor overemphasized. We have not yet managed to articulate a concept or a strategy for what should be a reasonable balance between risk and security, of which we have an outdated opinion. It seems we have not understood either one of them: to what extent is risk at the heart of our societies, and can we make use of a conception of security formulated in another era? That is why our feelings about fear are especially vulnerable. Dealing with a future with uncertain dangers is one of the most difficult things we have to learn: we are often fearful when there is not sufficient cause while we are unreasonably reckless at other times.

For classic authors on sociology such as Parsons or Durkheim, uncertainty had negative repercussions, irregularities that needed to be reoriented toward security. We are currently broadening our thinking so that uncertainty is understood as a possibility that generates the flexibility and learning ability that is essential in an innovation society. It is illusory to think that uncertainties or insecurities can be completely known and calculated. Given the complexity of social systems, we have a hard time when it comes to identifying and reducing insecurities. That is why we need a new culture of insecurity as a type of "third way" between risk aversion and recklessness, a way that explores the possibility of recuperating a functional equivalent of complete security through the construction of confidence, regulation, and cooperation.

When dealing with complex societies, where everything is tightly interrelated, the biggest question is how we can protect ourselves from our own irrationality. The chains of disaster events we need to guard against stem from our irresponsible tendency to fear too much or too little. During the economic crisis, for example, those who were managing financial innovations were less fearful than they should have been; now, distrust of economic agents can be explained because they may fear too much. Speaking in general terms, we should probably generalize a regulation ex ante, which would allow us to foresee things that cannot be remedied, anticipating rather than reacting, preventing rather than correcting. Furthermore, given that fears cannot be entirely eliminated, we need new strategies to govern them. That is why institutions exist; one of the functions of good government is to generate confidence and predictability, not allowing fear to turn to panic or boldness to favor irresponsibility.

Contemporary societies confront the crucial question of how to determine the relationship between risk and security again. The search for procedures to manage risks in an effective and socially acceptable manner has become a task of particular interest both for political reflection and for the practice of governance.

What role does politics play in this context? Concretely, what political innovations are required in a society that depends enormously on technological innovations but that also knows their undesirable consequences, in ecological, economic, and social terms, or regarding the values of freedom and justice?

POLITICS, FACING DANGER ALONE

In our collective imagination, technology appears as a potential threat. This suspicion stems from the fact that, not long ago, both the Right and the Left conceived of technology as a strong, successful, and incontestable reality. Some people hoped that political matters could be resolved (or even eliminated) thanks to the vision of experts and the accuracy of their procedures. Others bemoaned this process of technocratic depoliticization that would result in control, manipulation, destruction, and homogenization. In any case, the assessments would come after agreeing that this increased technification of the world would eventually prevail. To cite just one example of pessimistic premonition, we all remember Lane's (1966) warning that we were at the beginning of a new era in which scientific knowledge would reduce the significance of politics.

Today's reality is quite different: in addition to techniques that have been beneficial, we are surrounded by others that have failed. Some of the cases today have made us ever more conscious of the man-made risks that are increasingly out of control. Oil spills in the Gulf of Mexico, the economic crisis produced in large part by the failure of sophisticated technological financial products, and climate change induced by our development model are not only disasters with serious social repercussions but, from the outset, full-blown technological failures. In view of these failures, we can conclude that the technocrats were mistaken, but so were those who feared the success of technology rather than its failures.

What is interesting in this historical turmoil is that it has radically modified our way of understanding the articulation between politics and technology. Neither the technocratic Right nor the neo-Marxist Left of the 1960s and 1970s thought that the renovation of politics would ever stem from the failure of technology. What they imagined instead was its triumphant ascent, regardless of the consequences, whether it was celebrated or feared. The criticism of the technocracy is currently being suppressed by the fact that our technology is generally clumsy and diverse actors are constantly appealing for political intervention. We were hoping politics would protect us from the power of technology, but it now turns out that politics is being called on to resolve problems generated by technology's weakness.

Far from turning politics into an anachronism, technology (or, rather, its resounding failures or its potential risks) has reinforced the prestige of politics, which is now expected to provide what other actors have not. That is why it is no exaggeration to assert that managing these risks can be a new source of the legitimacy of political action (Czada 2000). It is still open to debate whether politics knows how to successfully exercise this responsibility and whether it has the necessary tools.

In this way, then, politics is making a comeback in three fundamental areas: the return of the state, the recuperation of political logic, and the demand for a democratic management of risks. Let us look briefly at each of these three points.

From the outset, disasters such as financial or environmental crises point toward a new form of regulatory state control. While the turn toward neoliberalism presumed a withdrawal of the state, the growing awareness of the dangers of a technological civilization encourages the state to assume new tasks, albeit in very different contexts than those in which it was used to acting sovereignly. It is not useful to be carried away on this point by what we could call a neo-Keynesian optical illusion: the state that is returning is not a rich sovereign state, but an indebted state in need of cooperation. The sooner we understand this new reality and explore possibilities for intervention, the less time we will waste on celebrating the fact that history has once again proven us right.

We can experience a moment of repoliticization specifically regarding the discrediting of the supposed experts. Those who monopolized accuracy and efficiency have failed; appealing to science and technology to put an end to controversies has become ideologically suspect; the world of the experts has been shown to be as rarely unanimous as our plural societies. All of that means that we are once again giving the political system the power to define the situation; we have an unusual opportunity to recover politics, in other words, we can employ the art of transforming our lack of evidence into decisions.

The management of risks, dangers, and disasters can also contain an element of democratization. A more uncertain world does not have to be less democratic than the disappeared world of certainties. Quite the opposite. One example of this could be the very evolution of the environmental movement. Ecological discourse, which was characterized in the 1970s by antistate discourse, has since begun to demand state regulation. The very fact of introducing environmental protection into the duties of the state opened a source of legitimacy for regulatory politics; in contrast, the so-called legitimacy of the welfare state, centered on the politics of redistribution, seems to have run its course. Subjecting technological risks to formal political procedures has introduced the conflict between economy and ecology into the system of government. It is no longer subversive or destabilizing. The development of Green parties, especially in Germany, is a telling example of this. After much discussion, the faction that preferred to join government coalitions has ended up imposing itself on the group that advocated external opposition. What some called "the ecological civil war" regarding nuclear energy did not lead to the overthrow of political authorities in the Federal Republic of Germany, as many had feared or hoped. The ecologists, who were arguing for an end to the state monopoly on violence at the beginning of the 1980s, came to recognize in 2000 that their goals could only be achieved through politics and the law.

It can thus be affirmed that while previous disasters could be the gateway to undemocratic states of emergency, the conflicts of "risk societies" have had a democratizing function and have encouraged a political culture of dialogue and conflict resolution. Our way of conceiving how to confront dangers in a democratic society is clearly differentiated from the authoritarian license that sovereign states grant themselves in order to resolve emergency situations. The dangers of the "risk society" do not require a state of emergency in the traditional sense. What they do require is as much normality as possible when handling threats. There are occasionally emergency situations in a democracy, and what we want is for them to be taken care of so we can return to a state of normality. For the reactionary jurist Carl Schmitt, on the other hand, the state of emergency does not arise from the disaster but from the battle against it. For Schmitt, the supreme power determines in a sovereign fashion if there is a state of emergency or not. This is more than a theoretical distinction: what distinguishes the democratic management of contemporary disasters from authoritarian sovereignty is precisely the concern for normality.

We are, therefore, faced with a strange paradox: politics has not been strengthened by technological perfection, but by its failure. Technology needs political regulation now more than ever. Advances in science have expanded political territory since they have produced new normative regulations and requirements. When technological failures are perceived as serious threats to the rights of citizens, there is a demand for politics to assume responsibility for creating the conditions that allow us to confront those consequences as a society. Without the resources of democratic legitimation and functioning states (now also in the form of global governance), there is no way to confront the insecurities, dangers, and accidents that modern technologies present.

We previously believed that there would be a technological solution for every problem in the future, but our response is now reversed and more modest: we can now be reasonably certain that the problems generated by technology will either be resolved politically or not at all.

4

A WALLED WORLD

THE current transformation of many of our borders into walls is a clear indicator of the ambiguity of the process of globalization, which combines opening and fragmentation, delimitation and closure. This issue places crucial aspects of our humanity at stake since borders and boundaries are linked to the realities of inside and outside, inclusion and exclusion, questions of identity and difference. The current tendency of multiplying strategies for closure reveals that we have significant difficulties when it comes to different ways of configuring everything that has to do with the legal-political realm, citizenship, identity, or security. Perhaps it is time to consider the opportuneness of a different way of conceiving the border. We could stop thinking of it as a wall and let it be a place of recognition, communication, and demarcation.

THE MULTIPLICATION OF WALLS

We were so absorbed with celebrating the coming of an unlimited world, the open spaces of globalization, the indetermination of the Internet, the freedoms of movement and communication, the new language of interdependence and soft power that we have been slow to recognize the flip side of this reality: a reterritorialized or even walled world, the fragmented space of multiculturalism, protectionisms, the proliferation of gated communities, and physical barricades. Our tributes to the memory of borders should consider whether we are not in fact facing their multiplication and displacement. The world that we label as global reveals a strange ambiguity since it is open, liberalized, and without boundaries, but, probably as a reaction to the foregoing, it also employs strategies of retreat, vigilance, and protectionism.

It is also true that the experience of boundaries and the transgression of boundaries are shared very unevenly, in an asymmetrical fashion. First of all, entering or leaving a territory, which is a mere formality for some citizens, can be a true impossibility or a struggle against the instruments of scrutiny and control for others. Different people have different experiences with borders depending on who they are, where they are coming from, where they are going to, and the reason why they are traveling. All of this allows us to deduce that the rhetoric about a "borderless world" reveals the fantasies of the minority who enjoy a digital existence in a world in which existence itself is a constant struggle for many.

This contrast is most notable in the proliferation of walls after the end of that long physical and ideological barrier that was the Cold War. Since the collapse of the Berlin Wall in 1989, the construction of new walls has multiplied, as if it were a frenetic race to respond to a new lack of protection: between Mexico and the United States (in California, Arizona, New Mexico, and Texas), on the West Bank, between India and Pakistan, between Iraq and Saudi Arabia, between South Africa and Zimbabwe, between

Spain and Morocco (encircling the cities of Ceuta and Melilla), between Thailand and Malaysia, and so on. The list could be expanded if we count the walls that are being planned, such as the wall Greece wanted to construct on their border with Turkey. In spite of the predictions announcing that globalization would lead to the creation of a world without borders, the United States, India, and Israel alone have built a total of fifty-seven hundred kilometers of security barriers (Jones 2012).

What are these walls? What is their purpose or, at least, what are the reasons why they are built? These barriers are not meant to prevent the attack of other sovereign powers or enemy armies but to impede the movement of people; they are meant to confront persistent and disorganized forces rather than military or economic strategies; they are more post-, sub-, and transnational than international; they are a response to the disconnected flows of state sovereignties. Current walls do not respond to the logic of the Cold War; they are walls of protection. They indicate, more than anything, a lack of confidence in the face of the Other, the foreigner, and in that way, they say a great deal about the ambiguities of globalization. Barriers "do not separate the 'inside' of a sovereign, political or legal system from a foreign 'outside,' but act as contingent structures to prevent movement across territory" (Weizman 2007, 172). They are directed at the movement of goods and people; this movement is not generally spurred by external invasion, but by internal demand: labor, drugs, prostitution, and the like.

In this regard, I fully share Wendy Brown's (2009) thesis and her paradoxical explanation: what has led to the frenetic construction of walls is not the triumph but the weakening of state sovereignty. This observation contradicts the traditional dogma of sovereignty. From Carl Schmitt to Giorgio Agamben, sovereignty has been defined as the power to establish a state of exception, and a wall would be the most expressive image of this. This conception is based on the idea that extralegal or exaggerated forms of exercising power are expressions of sovereignty, when it is really just the opposite: they are manifestations of the failure of sovereign power. Today's walls do not indicate a strengthening of the nation-state of full late modernity; they are icons of its erosion. Like all hyperbole, they reveal perplexity, vulnerability, and instability at the very heart of what they are attempting to defend. They signal an incapacity to govern the powers freed by globalization. Resorting to the barrier and the blockade is a desperate attempt to remedy this ungovernability.

A wall is not so much a material thing but a mental reality that traces a line of separation between an "inside" that feels threatened and a threatening "outside," which is seen as an enemy, global, stereotypical, ubiquitous, and sometimes ghostly. Walls function as tranquilizing icons to the extent that they reestablish a clear distinction between the interior and the exterior, between friend and enemy, which is often made to coincide with national borders. All the processes of ghettoizing make use of this same logic when they segment the city in an invisible manner, thus destroying the city's ability to bring its inhabitants closer. Barriers restore a type of sovereign, visible, material, and delimited power in an environment, unsettling for some, in which power is presented as a weak, diffuse reality. Walls are a psycho-sociological answer to the blurring of the distinction between the interior and the exterior, accompanied by other distinctions that have become problematic, like the difference between the army and the police, criminals and enemies, war and terrorism, legality and nonlegality, public and private, self-interest and general interest.

The building of walls not only illustrates backward movement in the dream of a "global world," but testifies to underground tendencies of globalization that foster the return to certain types of "neofeudalization" in the world, a world in which the simultaneity of the global economy and psycho-political isolation is surprisingly compatible. It could even be argued that the defense of this compatibility has become an ideological goal of that synthesis between political neoliberalism and state nationalism found in certain new right-wing groups whose project could be summarized in the double goal of "the denationalization of economics and the renationalization of politics" (Sassen 1996, xii). We do not live in a limitless world, but in the tension between a geography of open markets that tends to wipe out borders and a territoriality of national security that tends to build them. There is no consistency between geoeconomic and geopolitical practices to balance the different agendas of business and security.

PSYCHOPATHOLOGY OF BOUNDARIES

We have known since Machiavelli that fortresses tend to be more harmful than useful (1987, 2.24). Walls project an image of jurisdiction and assured space, a spectacular physical presence that is contradicted by the facts: in general, they do not help resolve conflicts, and they hardly prevent movement. They complicate goals, they force the modification of itineraries, but as for prohibiting movement, they tend not to be very effective.

The proliferation of walls in the era of limitless spaces is another manifestation of the degree to which human beings cling to strategies that are historically outdated but that continue to be practiced in spite of their uselessness. We can think of fortifications that continued to be built as if no one was aware that new methods of warfare had made them completely superfluous. There are, for example, citadels that were constructed at times when they no longer made sense. One of the most absurd examples is Antwerp, which built an exterior wall surrounding the city nine miles away from the city itself, and this barrier ended up limiting the city's space. In this way, the city found itself penned in by its own defensive zones, lacking sufficient soldiers to defend the stronghold itself.

Of course, walls cannot help restore a weakened sovereign state in the heart of the international system. To their minimal effectiveness, one would now have to add their anachronism in the age of climate change, intelligent bombs, digital attacks, and global epidemics. Walls have an archaic nature in a fluid world; they are a monument to solidity in the midst of evanescence, a delimitation that contrasts with the indetermination of financial and communicative spaces, a static affirmation against generalized mobility, a gesture of isolation in an environment of interdependence, a simulation of a protective niche that seems to ignore everyone's common exposure to the same global risks. From the point of view of security, it has been especially clear for some time now that fortifications are completely obsolete as defensive measures (Hirst 2005). Security experts advise against the closure of territorial space. Therefore, strict delimitations, of which walls are the prime example, display sovereign power and control that they do not exercise, especially now.

The most telling example of this is found in immigration control, which increases or decreases based on factors that are not connected to the rigidity or porousness of borders. Immigration exists because there are differential opportunities or, if one prefers, because inequalities are currently perceived in a global context (Beck 2008). When one thinks that the establishment of barriers is the solution to the increase in the number of immigrants and refugees, it is because it was previously believed that the cause of these displacements was the flexibility of borders, which is fundamentally false.

If they are not fulfilling this function that is assigned to them, then what good are these borders that take on the form of walls? Their meaning is undoubtedly independent of their functionality. Given their lack of efficacy, we need to ask what psychological necessities are satisfied by their construction. The answer lies in the need for boundaries and protection for those who perceive themselves—often against all evidence—as "besieged societies" (Bauman 2002a). We should not be surprised in this day and age that some things serve a need other than that which is declared or other than it might seem. Regarding walls, it is clear that they immediately allude to the defense against assailants who come from a chaotic "outside," but they serve as instruments of identification and cohesion, responding to fear in the face of the loss of sovereignty and the disappearance of homogeneous cultures. In this way, a sinister equivalence is constructed between otherness and hostility, an equivalence that is also a misperception (the majority of the attacks that have taken place in the United States have come from domestic terrorists). It reaffirms the prejudice that democracy cannot exist except in closed, homogenous spaces.

This is, then, a question of applying physical remedies to psychological problems, a theatralization with effects that are more visible than real. A wall appears to offer security in a world in which the state's ability to protect has decreased notably, in which subjects are more vulnerable to global economic fluctuations and transnational violence. Everything that accompanies the convincing scenography of walls is simply a political gesture intended to make a segment of the electorate happy, suppressing the image of politically embarrassing chaos and substituting it with an image of comforting order (Andreas 2000, 144). Although it is often impossible to completely close the borders, it is worse to give the impression of doing nothing. "Building a barrier is the best way to do nothing while giving the impression of doing something"; in this way, there is "seductive political activity directed against a group of especially complex problems, for which it is impossible to provide a short term solution" (Bhagwati 1986, 148).

Walls would be iniquitous if they merely left unresolved the problems they attempt to delimit in such a simple fashion. But this is not the case: walls generate areas of nonlaw and disputes, aggravate many of the problems they attempt to resolve, exacerbate mutual hostilities, project internal failures toward the exterior, and preclude any confrontation of global inequities. Furthermore, when security is ostentatiously accentuated, a sense of insecurity is provoked at the same time. There is too much collateral damage to compensate for the weak protection that walls provide.

OLD AND NEW SECURITY

Precise borders, presenting an uninterrupted line, were a constituent element of the modern nation-state, which is defined as sovereign over a determined space. The border as a fixed, continuous line creates a closed and sacred space and delimits it in the face of others, making crossing difficult or impossible. Since the end of the eighteenth century, the control of borders has become a systematic strategy. Boundaries are marked, controlled by police, and defended militarily. State power is staged on the borderline, which is also the place of legitimate control, even if there is no concrete reason for suspicion. It is the place where the state is entitled to place everyone under equal suspicion.

Bauman reminds us that modernity was an enterprise meant to colonize space, as if it could be conquered and closed off, guarded and limited with "No Entry" signs. Wealth and power have traditionally been weighty, extensive, and immobile forces. They grew with their expansion in space and had to protect themselves by defending the very space they occupied. But liquids, unlike solids, can scarcely guarantee their shape. The fact that power has become extraterritorial is seen most clearly in the fact that space has lost its classic value as a barrier and protection. With the fluidification of space, the difference between close and far, as well as the difference between civilization and wilderness, has been partially suppressed. Space is no longer an absolute impediment to action; distances hardly count and lose strategic meaning. If all areas of space can be easily reached, then none of them is privileged over the others.

This is the context in which one can speak of a degree of failure or inefficiency in the politics of delimitation. New spaces and new ways of thinking neutralize what John Agnew (1994) called "the territorial trap of the modern geopolitical imaginary," which is constructed based on three problematic assumptions: that, as the concept of sovereignty suggests, states have exclusive power inside their territories; that domestic and international spheres are distinct; and that state borders define social boundaries.

The growing complexity and differentiation of boundaries in global politics contrast with the simplicity of our practices in relation to them. In contemporary society, boundaries are not necessarily found where the contemporary geopolitical imaginary established them. With the image of the net, society stops being interpreted as a machine or an organism, as it has habitually been beginning with Hobbes's *Leviathan* and continuing until the end of the twentieth century. It is no longer seen as a territorial body marked by clear boundaries. Nets do not know delimited spaces, but communicative connections, the infrastructural channeling of flows. That is why we should begin to think that boundaries are no longer where they once were, in that institutionalized place where one sovereignty ended and another began. As Balibar (1998, 217) affirms, borders are no longer at the borders.

That explains the uselessness of maintaining the strict distinction between interior and exterior spaces that was characteristic of modern politics. The new forms of global governance minimize the distinction between inside and outside, which has made it impossible to articulate notions of sovereignty, territory, and security (Walker 1993; Bigo 2006). The "age of space" that began with the Great Wall of China and culminated with the Maginot Line began its last phase with the fall of the Berlin Wall. The events of September 11 made manifest the fact that territory could no longer be employed as a security resource. "Strength and weakness, threat and security have become now, essentially, extraterritorial issues" (Bauman 2002b, 82).

This destabilization has led to an intuitive but not very intelligent response in the realm of security: turning an entire territory into a border zone, as the Americans did after 9/11, accentuating the post–Cold War tendency of diminishing military expenses and increasing the budget for border control. In this way, a step was taken toward the progressive blurring of the difference between the control of boundaries and the control of the interior. Everyone becomes a security agent. What we have here is the unintended consequences of particular security policies: an increase in the area of operations turns the threat into something ubiquitous and permanent.

But, then, how should we defend ourselves in an undelimited world? What is the difference between old and new security? First of all, it is useful to fully understand the logic of new threats. The new type of transgressor takes advantage of the fortresses of the network-society, using its opening, its technologies, the density of its connections. Security policies are no longer dominated by a clear distinction between criminal and military threats, between enemies and delinquents. Everything revolves around the struggle against "nonconventional threats."

In the face of this type of danger, a defense of boundaries is not very effective. Border control suffers from a weakness from the very beginning: it can only expel people at the border, which is ineffective in relation to our principal threats. In any case, the defense of boundaries is no longer the defense of a territorial line but the conquest of defensive positions that are dispersed throughout the net. In addition, security today is far from the borders, and the lines of defense can be very far from one's own territory. The lines of military defense are shifted toward a particular rearguard, reaching sources where dangers are supposedly emitted, at hot spots generated at the folds of globalization. That is why the general vulnerability produced by current global flows is not resolved by completely isolating ourselves from the outside but through procedures of cooperation and global governance that presume an active internalization of the outside.

THE FUTURE OF BORDERS

Boundaries and borders have not become obsolete, nor has the territorial moment disappeared completely, but all of this must be thought about in a different way. First, we must understand that the concept of the border or boundary is in the legal-political realm; it is not a natural or neutral practice. This concept can be used unthinkingly, which means forgetting the contingency of the political order and reifying it. With an impervious national discourse, we lose sight of the fact that cultures and identities, far from being immutable, are historic in nature and are constantly transformed by the incorporation of new elements. We have to get used to cultural diversity by reducing the drama of its juxtaposition. We need to favor the circulation of people by relaxing the most static aspects of contiguity.

Rigid delimitations are a primitive method of providing security, and walls are ineffective. The best antidote to the wall is the border, in other words, the recuperation of boundaries that define, establish thresholds of movement, and allow for recognition. What must be fought are not borders but walls. The fact is that borders have other uses that the security obsession tends to undervalue, including communication and demarcation.

Walls are more of a barrier than borders are. The border, on the other hand, is not only something that divides and separates; it also allows recognition and an encounter with the other; it is more liquid than solid, a place of movement, of economic transaction, and of exchange. Far from blocking, separating, and homogenizing, the border communicates. For some time now, all fields of knowledge (physics, biology, geography, economics, and even law) conceive of the border by linking it to an absolutized distinction between the inside and the outside.

The border is also a mechanism for establishing fields, which are not necessarily exclusive. Correctly understood, the border can be a demarcating instrument in a world that, because of its delimited nature, needs procedures for protection and balance. It is also important to apply the principle that we should defend ourselves from that from which it defends us and understand that any delimitation is contingent and compatible with other fields with whose limits it overlaps.

In the face of the nostalgia for the lost order that clamors for tight limits and barriers of exclusion, the vindication of a border that communicates, demarcates, balances, and limits can be a reasonable strategy for transforming the spaces of collision, closure, and sovereignty in porous areas of contact and communication (Martins 2007, 176). The alternative, in any case, is not between the border and its absence, but between rigid borders that continue colonizing a good part of our political imaginary and a net border that would allow us to conceive of the contemporary world as a multiplicity of spaces that are differentiated and intertwined, thus creating border points that are also points of movement and communication.

PART III

GOVERNING, OR THE ART OF TAKING CHARGE

5

THE OBSERVATION SOCIETY

POWER has always meant an ability to observe, conceal, and even conceal oneself. Seeing implies social control; generally, to the extent that the possibilities of observation are increased, the likelihood of being seen decreases. That is why power has always come with the construction of watchtowers and observatories, or with increased sophistication of society's observation techniques, like censuses and polls.

The search for power still motivates people in the world today and may even have improved the techniques of control, but in a knowledge and information society, the technology that makes these observational operations possible is equally at the disposal of the people being observed. Foucault (1975, 220) linked the exercise of power to continual individual vigilance; the reequilibrium that is currently taking place has to do with the fact that there is an increase in citizen supervision of the authorities and the technological ability to carry it out. What we have is a type of "civic panopticism" that has reversed the exercise of the discipline. The authorities play the role of passive subjects more than active observers, and citizens have gone from being mere spectators to distrustful guards. The space of new technologies is superimposed over traditional public space, meaning that the political scene is now under more observation, from up close and at every possible angle.

Representative democracy presumed an unequal ability between those who govern and those who are governed, but when information or general education is increased, this no longer holds true. In advanced societies, those who govern make themselves more vulnerable and dependent (Rosanvallon 2008, 61). Communication and information technologies make possible a democratic vigilance that was unthinkable at times of informational asymmetry. "The old mechanisms of government don't work in a society where citizens live in the same information environment as those in power over them" (Giddens 2002, 75). The observational society is a more vigilant society, which presents new demands for transparency, but it must learn to manage those open informational environments where the problem is no longer concealment as much as the interpretation of reality.

WE, THE GATECRASHERS

Any society that has become democratized creates a corresponding public space, in other words, it becomes an environment where there are new ideas about observation, vigilance, the desire for transparency, debate, and control. That is what happened when the nation-states emerged, and something analogous is taking place now with global space. In both cases, there is the hope of creating a center of free debate and publicity that will lead to public diplomacy and nourish and solicit public opinion. The analogy is only partially valid, and there is no use in thinking about global governance with the same categories that apply to the limited space of nation-states. There is no doubt that something very similar to a global public space is slowly taking shape because of the confluence between communicative possibilities and the spread of democratic values.

The phenomenon of WikiLeaks is an indication that the geostrategic and diplomatic corps is in no position to halt publication or to remain protected within the secrecy that had been their milieu until now. This does not mean that secrets or discretion will be completely abolished from world diplomacy, but they are being reduced because of the creation of an observational society that has at its disposal more and more instruments to discover what is taking place in the secret corridors of power. This process is the result of the unstoppable insertion of societies into the political scene.

Diplomacy, which has been a reserved space, a dominium of secrets, the last bastion for reasons of state, a space of immunity, the last refuge in the face of the assaults of democratization, is now found besieged by what we could call a right for societies to observe international affairs. We are moving toward a form of public diplomacy that breaks away from the traditional idea of secrets. By emerging on the international scene, societies modify diplomatic strategies in profound ways. From the beginning, internationalization presumes the growing visibility of social questions.

In a world where everyone sees one another, where everyone compares themselves, borders lose their capacity for delimitation and discretion. Societies do not only intervene with their respective governments; these convergences also place global spaces under social vigilance. The process of constructing the global public space can be understood, negatively, as a process by which subjects free themselves from the framework of the state. Social behaviors increasingly escape the framework of national socialization: opinions, values, likes and dislikes, investments, and behaviors are articulated beyond traditional institutional framing. We find ourselves in the midst of a series of dynamics whose complexity and interdependence are largely determined by the fact that "cross-cutting" structures, diverse actors, and furtive interests are all in play. This allows us to conclude that the concept of "us" that the states articulate does not correspond with social and economic realities.

The process of configuring a global public space points to the formation of a new subject, global humanity, which is the final judge of political practices. Because of globalization, the world has become a publicly observed space. Nonconformist dynamics have led societies to enter into international political debate. The global public space has created conditions that are expressed and addressed. Of course, we should not get our hopes too high. The opinion that appears on the international scene is not the ideal antiestablishment movement, an effective force that can challenge the power of the states. The supervisory function of societies barely prevents—there is no veto—but it does reconfigure the international game to the point of making arbitrariness extremely costly. This intrusion and vigilance already challenge the power game itself or the value of ignorance, which authorities have found very useful (Badie 2004). Fifteen million people took to the streets in February 2003. They did not manage to prevent the war in Iraq, but they contributed decisively to delegitimizing it. Up-to-date knowledge of "foreign affairs" is the first step to open these matters to debate where anyone can take a side without needing government approval or patriotic alignment. We live in a world that rejects the excuse of the secret, that would prefer to profoundly modify the sense of diplomacy in order to insert it into public discussion.

International politics has long benefited from the value of ignorance. States could allow themselves almost anything when what they were doing was barely known. The Soviet army coup in Budapest in 1956 met with less resistance than the coup twelve years later in Prague. There was television in European homes by that point, and the image of the tanks deployed by the Warsaw Pact nations helped forge the beginning of international public opinion. In recent years, the idea of a public diplomacy that could replace old secretive practices with marketing that would court public opinion has become more popular. This change of strategy corresponds to the fact that power is being actively observed by eagerly solicited opinion. It is increasingly more difficult to appeal to democracy without looking for the support of public opinion, without agreeing to abandon a part of one's own power to the game of collective deliberation.

The twentieth century has ended the monopoly that states enjoyed in their role as the only international actors. Such denationalization corresponds to the creation of a public space of free discussion and compromise at the heart of which we are all witnesses to genocides, law breaking, oppression of every kind, inequality, and so on. Globalization is also a space for public attention that notably reduces the distances between witnesses and actors, between responsible parties and spectators, between oneself and everyone else. New transnational communities of protest and solidarity are configured in this way. The new actors, to the extent that they watch and denounce, continue to destabilize the authorities' capacity to impose themselves in a coercive fashion. No state is the owner of its image. Observational society participates directly in the debate that the global public space founds and acts in the name of a universal legitimacy. In this way, no state can neuter the gaze that studies it. The turn taken in the discussion of international penal justice is very meaningful in this regard: we are moving from a system of justice dictated in the name of the people to a justice that appeals to humanity. The states' new international responsibility responds to the fact that humanity increasingly imposes itself as a reference to international action.

LIMITS TO TRANSPARENCY

The sign of our times is immediacy. Nothing is more suspicious to us than mediations, intermediaries, constructions, and representations. We think that if the facts are on hand we will know the truth, that democracy's only requirement is to have nothing impeding us from making a decision. In our collective unconsciousness (we also sometimes formulate this explicitly), we consider information more useful than interpretations and, by the same prejudice, we tend to believe it is more democratic to participate than to delegate. A similar lack of confidence in mediation leads us to automatically presume that things are true when they are transparent, that representation always falsifies, and that every secret is illegitimate. There is nothing worse than an intermediary. That is why we immediately feel closer to someone who leaks information than to a journalist, to an amateur than to a professional, to NGOs than to governments. For this reason, our greatest scorn is aimed at those who imply the greatest degree of mediation: as opinion polls remind us, our greatest problem is—the political class. At the rate we are going, it will also end up that their pensions are the cause of the economic crisis. The current fascination with social networks, participation, and proximity reveals that the only utopia still standing is disintermediation.

With this state of affairs, no one should have been surprised that WikiLeaks is viewed as a confirmation of what we already knew: that the system is terrible and that we are innocent. This coincides in time with an economic crisis whose commentators have been repeating for some time now that it is being paid for by those of us who did not cause it. Fortunately, we are not a part of the market that is dedicated to conspiring and attacking. Now that the problems have been identified and the responsibilities assigned, we have saved ourselves nearly the entire task of conceiving of a complex world and adapting democracy to new realities. Indignation can continue comfortably replacing reflection and democratic effort.

Transparency is, without a doubt, one of the principal democratic values. It allows citizens to control the activity of their elected representatives, to verify respect for legal procedures, to understand decision-making processes, and to trust political institutions. Thanks to the Internet, this transparency can be expanded in a new fashion since the data can be made public in a direct and anonymous fashion. However, are we so certain that having free access to 250,000 documents from American diplomacy makes us more intelligent and better democratic citizens? Would we know more about the world if all secrets were suppressed? Are we made into better citizens as we go about discovering the extent to which many of our authorities are clumsy and cynical?

We should not allow ourselves to be carried away by the idea that we are in a world where information is available, transparent, and secret-free. In the first place, because we are aware that certain successful past negotiations would not have taken place if they had been broadcast live. There is something that we could call the diplomatic benefits of nontransparency. Of course, in this arena, many traditional procedures are destined to disappear, and anyone who participates in a diplomatic process from now on must be aware that almost everything will end up coming to light. But it is also true that the demand for total transparency may often paralyze public action. There are compromises that cannot be achieved out in the open. Too much light can tend to make actors radicalize their positions. In spite of certain hurried celebrations of a forthcoming world without duplicity or shadows, the distinction between being on or off stage continues to be necessary for politics.

But there is also an ambiguity to naked, noncontextualized transparency. It is an illusion to think that making facts public is enough to make truth rule in politics, the authorities come clean, and citizens understand what is really going on. In addition to access to public data, there is the question of its meaning. Placing large quantities of data and documents on the Internet is not enough to make public action intelligible: they need to be interpreted, the conditions under which they were produced must be understood, and the fact that they generally do not represent more than a single segment of reality must be remembered.

Accessibility of information on the Internet does not guarantee its visibility. The transparency and access to documents are frequently invoked as a sure sign of an institution's democracy, but if you want to know what is going on, what documents should you request? (Weiler 1999, 349). Transparency is only real if those who govern, in addition to making facts available, provide information. This brings us back to the problem of mediation, which was what we thought we could overcome. It is tricky to look at the Internet with the categories of traditional public space thinking that everything here is public and everything is information (Cardon 2010). For something to be public, it is not sufficient that it be accessible; for information to exist, there must be a specific elaboration of facts. This indeterminacy expresses the greatness of the Web, but also its limitations.

In addition to limits, transparency can have perverse effects. Many people have noted that the Internet can become an instrument for opacity: the increase of facts provided to citizens complicates their job of vigilance (Fung, Graham, and Weil 2007). Any piece of information we are incapable of understanding would make us like Aeschylus's characters who "had vision but saw nothing" (1985, 73). It is opacity and not the lack of transparency that most impoverishes democracies. Obsessing about transparency and neglecting everything else are the same as erring on where to focus attention. Our biggest enemy is not secrets, concealment, or intrigues, but banality.

In this regard, it is worth mentioning something surprising that makes political reality unintelligible, not because we lack facts or because we do not scrutinize our representatives carefully enough, but because we do so excessively, constantly, and instantaneously. Extreme vigilance of political actors can make them overprotect their actions. One example of this is the fact that many politicians, knowing that their smallest acts and declarations are examined and shared, tend to put their communications in a straitjacket. Democracy today is more impoverished by speeches that say nothing than by the express concealment of information.

Democratic societies are right to demand greater and simpler access to information. But the abundance of facts does not guarantee democratic vigilance; for that, we also need to mobilize communities of interpreters capable of giving a context, meaning, and critical assessment. Separating the essential from the anecdotal, analyzing, and situating facts within an adequate framework require intermediaries who have time and cognitive competencies. Political parties are an essential instrument to reducing that complexity. In this task of interpreting reality, journalists are also inevitable. Their job is not going to be superfluous in the age of the Internet. Quite the opposite. Journalists are bound to play an important role in this cognitive mediation to interest people, animate public debate, and decipher the complexity of the world (Rosanvallon 2008, 342). But I am defending the cognitive necessity of the political system and the means of communication and not its representatives who, like everyone, can also clearly be improved.

We should not underestimate interpretative challenges in a world of fluctuations where there is excessive information while our understanding is overwhelmed, saturated, and disoriented. Commenting on and interpreting reality are not something that just anyone can do well, as promised by the dream that bloggers themselves will begin producing information. Validating, interpreting, and communicating information demand competence and responsible actions.

Defending this task of mediation today is like renouncing the easy pleasure of floating downstream: almost no one wants to renounce the possibility of expressing indignation that is found in the possibility of killing the intermediary. In the face of all the promises of interpretative patience, the Internet is a space that offers direct participation and democracy, expression and decision without intermediaries. All of which is linked with the democratic distrust toward the expert and the resulting celebration of the common citizen who seems democratically unobjectionable. The freedom of the amateur in contrast to the restrictions of the professional: this is the new conflict for which the Internet constitutes a formidable battleground (Leadbeater and Miller 2000; Keen 2008;

Flichy 2010). Some people even celebrate the appearance of new amateur journalists who might come to replace the professionals. The presence of the amateur, of the scandalized leaker, is very important and doubtlessly helps democratize the process of the creation and circulation of information. But in reality, there is a much more complex network of cooperation between them: only the great papers have the ability necessary to make use of those mountains of information. A specific sign that transparency was not the only thing that was in play is the fact that the leak was negotiated, with exclusivity granted to a limited group of papers.

In the end, we end up needing mediation, professionalism, and representation. Without them, the world is less intelligible and more ungovernable. We will need to judge whether these conditions do what they need to do well and not allow ourselves to be trapped by the lazy illusion that their mere lack will make us free.

SECRETS ARE ELSEWHERE

The fact that we live in a complex society is another way to refer to the fact that things have become very confusing for us. Our unlimited possibilities for observation and information are not proportionate to our limited ability to gain a coherent idea of the world, knowing where the most important things are and unmasking unjustified concealment. This opacity is due to the fact that the distribution of power is more volatile, the determination of causes and responsibilities is more complex, presences are virtual, and enemies are diffuse. Society understands itself less and less from the visible actions of individuals or concrete groups; it is established as an intrigue beginning with interactions that are complex and difficult to recognize.

In a democracy, this opacity is not welcomed as good news but as something that, in principle, should be fought. The birth of modern democracy includes suspicion toward power and especially toward hidden power. We tend to think that the state is always tempted to abuse its prerogatives, that it protects by invoking excessive confidentiality, and that it only affords information that does not put itself at risk. Our political institutions and practices have been formed through this tension; they have been confronted with demands for transparency and publicity. We should not be surprised by citizens' suspicion or by the state's invocation of secrets, because both are part of the political debate in a democratic society.

It is striking that we look at reality with just one eye, in a manner of speaking. We scrutinize the political system so closely, but our scrutiny of the economic world is superficial, even though we make transcendental decisions there, presuming optimal conditions of information and transparency. Opacity in politics and transparency in the economy? If the economic crisis has revealed anything, it is that this contrast is not true, that it is even the result of a deliberate ideological maneuver, because our permanent observation of politics contrasts with the elevated clandestineness that economic agents have enjoyed. In fact, even though there is always room for improvement, the opacity of the states is not as solid as sometimes bemoaned, and the transparency of the markets is not as effective as some people proclaim.

In the first place, any state should submit to a series of rules to communicate its decisions, whether it is in the present moment (because of the obligation of publicity and in order to create statistical instruments to explain its actions) or in a delayed fashion (by creating archives and making them available). Internal controls and evaluations, guarantees of democracy, strict regulation of official secrets and reserved materials, vigilance of the means of communication, the evaluation of public policy, all of this feeding a never-ending wave of scrutiny, criticism, and counter-arguments. Rankings, reports, and statistics provide information about states that are barely in control of their own image anymore. If that were not enough, states are observed by others (in an especially intense way in the case of the European Union, where, because of the interdependencies and mutualization of sovereignty, they are forced to at least be aware of the impact of their decisions on other states). The state is also probed by economic actors, who assess fiscal policies or weigh their level of risk. The state can barely escape from the demand to make its actions and ways of operating public. As Castells (2003) notes, the state today is more observed than observer. Long gone are the times when political actors had the privilege of looking without being seen; they are now subjected to continuous and unlimited observation.

We shall see what is taking place in areas we tend not to observe. In contrast, economic opacity has not stopped growing in recent years. It is true that market functionality requires transparency in principle. Economic actors can only adopt correct decisions if their predictions are well founded, in other words, if they dispose of all the information necessary to limit the amount of change involved in their decisions. However, since the 1980s, economic theory has tried to explain situations of distortion or asymmetry of information that falsify relations between actors and the possibility of a general equilibrium of the market. This inequality is even more contingent in the financial markets or when the contagion effects of opinions or self-fulfilling prophecies turn information into a weapon in the economic war. We have seen this with the financial crisis: the sophistication of financial products has created an uncontrolled complexity that feeds risks capable of destabilizing economic life as a whole.

I am not only referring to the fact that deregulation has allowed the resourceful use of uncontrolled areas: banking secrets, tax havens, over-the-counter markets, dark pools, and so on. These could all be viewed as exceptional cases. The most serious problem is that there is structural opacity: given that credit derivatives, for example, are based on other financial instruments and often combine various additional risks, the potential for loss cannot be fully measured. The dynamics of innovation in global finances entail a string of risks that can increase general risk through unknown hidden influences and combined effects. Securitization has acted as a global mechanism for a lack of responsibility, which disseminated and concealed risks, introducing securities into the markets with risks that no one was able to evaluate. The development of new, exotic, illiquid financial instruments, the growth of increasingly complex derivatives, and the fact that many financial institutions are opaque or little regulated have all contributed to the general lack of transparency. This opacity has destroyed the confidence of investors. The difficulty of evaluating prices, risks, or toxicity has turned into general uncertainty. In the end, it turned out that with certain financial products, people did not know exactly what they were buying and the risks they were assuming.

It is not surprising that we are only now, with a delay, noticing the extent to which the economic crisis stemmed from measurements and calculations that presumed exactitude that they were not in any position to provide (Charolles 2008; Beauvallet 2009). There are more and more voices that warn of the inherent limits of any modeling and that question the supposedly absolute trustworthiness of the measuring systems or the preciseness of previsions.

Current mistrust can be interpreted as a reaction of investors against an opaque financial system, whose scope they do not fully understand. "The mathematical complexity of financial innovation and transactions has been running ahead not only of the ability of regulators to follow (much less to control a priori) but also of the ability of many firms . . . to understand" (Cerny 1994, 331). The economy is not, of course, a simple reality, but when the inevitable complexity becomes suspicious opacity, actors become blocked and markets stop functioning. We could talk in this case about ideologically produced opacity. The very fact of presenting financial affairs as something excessively technical and complex has facilitated a transfer of authority toward the supposed experts and has devalued the authority of those who govern. This has depoliticized these affairs and removed relevant decisions from public discussion.

It is not fair that the vigilance of the world is so poorly divided. If the economy were subjected to the same degree of observation as politics, that in itself would make things run much better. When will there be a WikiLeaks for the markets? For lack of a better term, this is another name for global economic governance.

UNRAVELING AN ILLUSION

For years now, the Internet has been provoking illusions of democratization that do not fully correspond with the results. We were told to expect accessibility of information, the elimination of secrets, and the dissolving of power structures, in such a way that it seemed inevitable to advance with the democratization of society, renewing our tedious democracy or implanting it in societies that seemed protected in the face of the most beneficial effects of the Internet. The results do not seem to be on a par with what was announced, and the first theories of this disillusionment that are attempting to problematize the myth of digital democracy are now being formulated. This resistance to adjusting promises to fit possibilities is probably very human, so we oscillate between expectations and disappointment, before figuring out what it is reasonable to expect.

The illusion that nurtures all technological innovation is also very human. Social utopia is part of the emergence of technologies, and history is full of exaggerated dreams raised by technical possibilities. Marx believed that the train would destroy the caste system in India; the telegraph was presented as the definitive end of prejudices and hostilities between nations; some people celebrated the airplane as a means of transportation that would suppress not only distances, but also wars; similar dreams accompanied the birth of the radio and television. We now contemplate those assumptions with scorn and irony, but in their moment, they afforded a sense of promise.

The technologies to which we owe the current deployment of social networks have not been isolated from this phenomenon, in this case, additionally, with good reason. It is logical that a technology that empowers, freely connects, and facilitates access to knowledge awakens illusions of democratic emancipation. The anarchist-liberal story of the founders of the Internet has been retold by people of every ideological persuasion, on the Right and on the Left. Digital optimists have always overestimated the democratizing effect of the free circulation of information, which is the reputation it acquired with the fall of the communist regimes. On the other hand, old-fashioned hippies ended up at universities and technological centers trying to prove that the

Internet could provide what the 1960s promised: greater democratic participation, individual emancipation, a strengthening of community life, and so on.

Once the exaggerated expectations are overcome, we are in a position to unravel this illusion and ask ourselves if the Internet has truly increased the public sphere and the extent to which it has made new forms of participation possible, increasing the power of the people in the face of the elites. Without ignoring the Internet's capabilities, we can critically examine the promises of cyber-utopianism, that ingenuous belief in the inexorably emancipatory nature of online communication that is unaware of its limits or even its dark side. It seems to me that these errors can be synthesized around the conceptions of technology, power, and democracy that underlie the dream of digital democracy. We frequently understand technology in a deterministic manner, without taking its social context sufficiently into account; cyberspace is conceived as an area where power disappears; we praise the destabilizing function of the Web in relation to repressive systems without paying enough attention to the constructive dimension of democracy.

For the concrete case of information and communication technologies, it is also valid to say that the enthusiasm for technology has simplified the vision of its political effects, exaggerated its possibilities, and minimized its limitations. Much of our perplexity about the limits or ambiguities of the social processes made technologically possible is due to not having understood that any technological innovation is carried out in a social context and has social effects that vary according to the context in which they are deployed. Technological determinism tends to think of its users as passive subjects of transferred technology and not as people who appropriate it in their own ways.

Information does not flow in a void but in a political space that is already occupied, organized, and structured in terms of power (Keohane and Nye 1998). If we would have kept this in mind, we would not have been naïve enough to think that a technology as sophisticated as the Internet would produce identical results in different countries. We would know that the Internet puts into motion dynamics that increase uncertainty around the path that societies will take, both in consolidated democracies and in authoritarian regimes.

Social networks are, of course, a democratizing factor, but many other things as well. Not having understood that the logic of technology varies from one context to another, we have not adequately assessed the effect of the Internet on authoritarian regimes and its unforeseen consequences. Western observers have assumed that dictators could not use the Internet in their favor because they thought that the Internet's decentralization of power was a universal phenomenon, a rule without exception, and not a rule specific to our democracies.

The other principle that has been assumed claimed that global networks constitute a movement that is contrary to the concentration of power, that they destabilize the authority of the elites and tend to quash established imbalances (Castells 2011, 136). However, to what extent is the Internet's structure so open? Is it true that citizens are listened to more closely in cyberspace, that networks decentralize audiences, favor the flexibility of organizations, and allow for the disintermediation of political activity? It may be that the mechanisms of exclusion have changed, but this does not mean they have disappeared. The "gatekeepers" (who leak on information channels and condition our decisions) are still part of our social and political landscape. There are those who even claim that there is greater audience concentration on the Internet than through traditional means of communication (Hindman 2009). There is not necessarily more objectivity or less partisanship in the open space of the Internet than in the space of traditional media. The fact that power is decentralized or more diffuse does not mean that there is less power, that we are freer, or that there is higher-quality democracy.

The Internet does not eliminate power relationships, but it transforms them. The great opening-up of the Internet is what, paradoxically, has contributed to the creation of new elites. It is well known that the most influential blogs in the United States do not represent much social plurality (almost all of them belong to middle- or upper-class white men). There continue to be imbalances on the Web; it is naïve to think that the Internet always and necessarily favors the oppressed over the oppressor. It is true that new technologies allow a type of "monitorial citizenship" (Schudson 1999), a critical vigilance on the part of the public that has democratizing effects, but there are also phenomena of "crowdsourcing" censorship, of regressive vigilance in which Internet actors can participate. In fact, there is increasingly more censorship carried out by intermediaries than by governments, and this censorship takes on commercial rather than strictly political forms.

But the most important reason behind the persistence of power relationships on the Internet is structural; it is found in its very design. To understand the infrastructure of power on the Internet, we must keep in mind that its connective nature determines the content that citizens see, in virtue of which not all choices are equal. The Internet follows a "winner take all" logic that has profound implications in terms of inequality (Lessig 1999). This is not due to norms or laws but to the decisions that are found in the very design of the Internet, which determines what users are or are not allowed to do. The topology link that regulates the traffic on the Web makes the Internet somewhat less open than what was hoped or feared. There is a structural hierarchy because of "hyperlinks," an economic hierarchy of the big corporations like Google or Microsoft, and a social hierarchy because a certain type of professional is overrepresented on forums for online opinions.

The Internet contains a concentration of search engine providers. They appear as simple mediators or claim to limit themselves to reflecting existing traffic, but they also direct and condition the traffic. The Web allows for the proliferation of pages and places, but in fact, search engines centralize the attention of the public in such a way that interactions are more limited than we tend to believe and the number of places we visit is smaller than we presume. What causes this?

It is due to the fact that the options are strictly predefined, and they sometimes set aside more important alternatives. Although it is in principle possible for individuals to control these options, only a minority of people is capable of doing so. "Google's great trick is to make everyone feel satisfied with the possibility of choice, without actually exercising it to change the system's default settings" (Vaidhyanathan 2011, 2157–2163). With this in mind, it is not too much to affirm that current cultural imperialism is a question not of content but of protocols. What is in play here is the question of the neutrality of the Web: the influence that is exercised on users is not in the content but in the framework. It is at this level where our ways of searching and finding, exploring and buying are structured. It is a matter of an influence that conditions our habits with a nudge and that, to that same extent, can be considered an ideological expression. The supreme value of this ideology is "free expression," and it carries a suspicious similarity to the values of deregulation, freedom of circulation, and transparency, all understood in a neoliberal fashion. It is because of this that these values are hard to assume in other cultures, but also in democratic countries that, like France and Germany, try to impede access, for example, to anti-Semitic pages.

Digital activism is already a few years old, and it affords us some experience. The most important is that we must distinguish the critical and destabilizing function from the ability for democratic construction. The example of the Arab revolts reveals that tearing down is not building, that decentralization is not sufficient for the success of political reforms. The fact that Barack Obama was better as a candidate than he is as president should serve to control the fascination that the Internet has exercised on those who seem to have forgotten that winning elections is not the same as governing, in the same way that communicating well is not equivalent to making opportune decisions.

For the transformation of authoritarian systems, the indispensable presence on the Internet can even be ineffective and illusory. Morozov has criticized this "cloud activism" (2011, 170) that can end up implying scorn for practice, for other forms of social action as important for democratization as the physical occupation of spaces. The relative "comfort" of the digital world can make mobilization take the place of organization (Davis 2005).

The fact that the Internet is ripping down barriers, weakening the power of institutions and intermediaries, should not make us forget that institutions must function smoothly in order to allow for the preservation of freedom. This is the reason that the Internet can facilitate the destruction of authoritarian regimes but is not as effective when it comes to consolidating democracy.

Access to the instruments of democratization is not the same as the democratization of a society.

Those who are in favor of social networks often forget that if an authoritarian government loses control over its people, that does not mean that it will inevitably be replaced by democracy. A failed state can be worse than an authoritarian one. The power of the Internet linked with the incompetence of a weak state is the precursor of anarchy and injustice.

We could conclude with the evidence that the emergence of the Internet is going to profoundly modify politics, which can no longer be practiced as it has been. At the same time, we should not slip into the type of digital sanctimoniousness that seems unaware of its contradictions. The fact that the Internet is based on simplicity and confidence also constitutes its vulnerability; it facilitates resistance, criticism, and mobilization, but it exposes us to new risks in new ways.

Certain phenomena like the financialization of the economy or the spread of errors are also part of the face of the Internet that some call dark, but that I would prefer to call risky. However, when have human beings had an instrument whose emancipatory capabilities did not also include possibilities of self-destruction? Governing specifically means fomenting emancipatory capabilities while preventing or impeding self-destructive ones.

6

FROM SOVEREIGNTY TO RESPONSIBILITY

A world that belongs to everyone and to no one is a world that must be conceived and governed with categories other than those applied to the nation-state. Must we abandon the idea of a world that is organized in accordance with democratic values and principles of justice or can we imagine democracy on a global scale? Is intervention in "other people's" affairs legitimate or are we compelled to accept anything that is carried out in the name of sovereignty? Are there criteria for global justice or must we accept that justice is a value that only measures relationships within states? These three notions—democracy, humanism, justice—must be deliberated within a new context that can be synthetized in the belief that we need to move from sovereignty to responsibility.

DEMOCRACY BEYOND NATIONS

Let us presume, even though it may be presuming too much, that nations are democratic or that, at the very least, we know how democratic institutions are created and developed within the framework of the nation-state. What happens, then, when we talk about institutions beyond nations, such as the European Union or truly international institutions? In these arenas, is it possible and desirable for decisions to be made democratically or are we forced to surrender to the impossibility of such a task? Most importantly, what happens when the importance of the decisions that are made in these arenas that escape the limits of the nation-state increases?

We have a problem here, perhaps the most serious problem that humanity's current political organizations are confronting. Globalization is depoliticized, that is, it flows without direction or in a nondemocratic direction, pushed by ungovernable processes or by unaccountable authorities. Numerous decisions are distanced from the space of democratic state responsibility, which complicates questions of legitimacy and acceptance. There are more and more intrusive politics that the public struggles to understand and accept (for example, military interventions that stem from the responsibility to protect people or the control of the economies of countries with which we share a common destiny). How are pressures on speculative markets, prohibitions against certain countries developing particular weapons, or European demands for budgetary austerity democratically justified? Who has the right to tell Greece, Syria, or Iran what they must do?

The problem becomes more serious as institutions that only weakly correspond to our criteria of democratic legitimation acquire growing importance. International institutions are essential for the solution of certain political problems, but they are structurally nondemocratic if we apply the criteria by which we measure the democratic quality of a nation-state. This set of circumstances immediately awakens a logical sense of dissatisfaction, as we can see from the high degree of indifference toward politics, local and global protests, hopelessness about politics' ability to carry out authorized governmental tasks under current circumstances, and, more concretely, a lack of identification with international institutions and the European Union, which are especially vulnerable to populism.

Now, we have proof that those who are unsatisfied are not always right since some proposed solutions are even more unsatisfactory than the detected problems. Protests point in the right direction—transparency, participation, democratic control—but they are flawed when they are unable to imagine another form of legitimacy than could be used for spaces and decisions that are no longer in the arena of the nation-state and are very unlikely to return to this well-known territory. At the beginning of the failed Constitutional Treaty for Europe, there was a desire to end the "permissive consensus" and reactivate a politicization that could only come from explicit citizen approbation.

Considering this state of affairs, no one can be surprised that there is little identification with the process of European integration. It is accused of not fulfilling democratic demands that, apparently, member states satisfy perfectly. Both the Right and the Left are generally moving back toward a safe space, whether that is in relation to national identity or to social protection. Depending on their ideological sensibilities, people will be more concerned about one thing or another, but in any case, a return to old references and a general rejection of any form of political experimentation seem to be unavoidable.

This movement back toward known quantities was crystalized with the German Constitutional Court's ruling on the Treaty of Lisbon of 2009, when national democracy was taken as the model to assess the legitimacy of the European Union, as if the court did not appreciate the institutional novelty represented by the Union. It demanded democratic control of power without taking into account the other side of the coin: achieving and safeguarding democracy now requires institutions capable of acting beyond the nation-state. The court also reclaimed German organizational control over European agencies. If something similar were done by the other member states, decisions would be blocked at the European level.

Jürgen Habermas wrote an article that principal European newspapers published in October 2011. His position was unmistakably federal, but the effects justify the return to the national arena. In it, he coined the phrase "postdemocratic Europe" to refer to the current situation of the European Union, which he believes is monopolized by elites and by market imperatives without democratic legitimation (Habermas 2011). The proliferation of "technological" or political governments that justify themselves with accounting criteria rather than with explicit democratic standing seemed to corroborate the accusation. Habermas's way of thinking is tired: opaque elites versus democratic people, the system as opposed to the lifeworld. As if citizens knew exactly what needs to be done and how, while our political leaders do not know what to do and would not be capable of carrying it out.

Does this dilemma have a solution that is neither cynical nor populist? Is there a third way between technocracy and demagogy? Robert Dahl (1994) synthesized politics' fundamental dilemma in the age of globalization as the contradiction between the effectiveness of the system and citizen participation. With this, he was referring to two fundamental types of legitimation in which to ground our institutions and political practices: the legitimacy that comes from popular support or accepting decisions based on democratic procedures (input legitimacy) and the legitimacy that is acquired from the capacity of securing public goods and resolving problems of economic globalization (output legitimacy).

It is true that the purely functional, apolitical justifications of international institutions and the European Union are insufficient (Zürn and Ecker-Ehrhardt 2012). It is not acceptable that the elites from a few countries, discounting national and global public opinions, condition the national politics of other countries. However, the impact of international political decisions on domestic spaces is not always an unjust intervention, but a reality that is ever more present and that requires legitimation. Something similar is taking place with the spread of technological criteria in current politics and even with "technocratic" governments. Technological competence is a fundamental requirement for good politics and not paying attention to it tends to activate a desperate call for efficiency as the last resort. These types of situations are most assuredly only justifiable under exceptional circumstances and in a provisional manner.

In any case, our democratic ideal would be completely illusory if we thought about it as a permanent plebiscite, without any delegation of any type, without other people's interventions. If democracy could not be anything but popular and close, if it were unthinkable beyond the spaces and in matters for which self-determination is possible and desirable, then we could say goodbye to adventures beyond the nation-state and return—if this were possible—to simpler societies and to delimited spaces. Paradoxically this desertion would not help resolve global problems with better democratic criteria but would, quite simply, abandon them to their fate, which is as undemocratic as a situation can be.

Therefore, in the era of politics beyond national borders, of interdependence and networks, functional legitimation is bound to acquire greater importance regarding territorial representation. The political system has to respond to the expectation that we live in "societies that resolve problems" (Scharpf 1997). For this affirmation not to presume a desertion of the principles that rule our democratic societies, the emphasis on functionality demands a differentiation of scope because it cannot have the same weight on neighboring affairs as it does for global problems or in the temporal register of urgency as it does for constitutional provisions. The presence of disputed and seemingly contradictory principles is part of our political condition, but one must know how to adequately manage things based on the problem in question and the circumstances conditioning it.

In the current situation, we cannot progress toward necessary European federalization with any confidence in the support of inhabitants who do not understand the European structure, people who have been bombarded for years with protectionist speeches and who are now being served an image of Europe as a disciplinary agent at the service of the markets, without remembering the responsibilities we share and the mutual advantages we receive. We find the appeal to a sovereign people or the recourse to the criticism of our leaders intellectually and politically very comfortable. It makes us feel morally irreproachable as a member of the innocent crowd. Someone should remind us, however, that there would be no populist leaders if there were not populist peoples.

It is not terribly realistic to think about transposing the categories of nation-state democracies to processes like the European Union or especially to global governance. David Held suggests that if we want to talk about global democratization we need to be less strict with the criteria of democraticity than we tend to be when we talk about democratic states. It is reasonable to understand that in global processes "there is little room for democracy... but a lot of space for legitimacy" (Willke 2007, 127).

From this perspective and with all these nuances, we should revise the platitude that democracy is only realizable within the framework of the nation-state. Schumpeter's (1942) idea that the success of a democracy depends on not extending the range of political decision too far rests on past experience, but it seems to invite us to abandon current global processes for a way of thinking that is opposed to any idea of just government.

In the end, the problem is not whether global arenas do or do not allow for a democracy similar to the one that is configured in nation-states, but how to overcome the incongruence between social and political spaces. What is most essential is that there be legitimate government or governance and not whether democratic requirements that only serve, strictly speaking, for delimited spaces can be extended globally. In this sense, international institutions (as well as the European Union, which is not truly an international organization but something more intense) make it possible for politics to recover the capacity for action in the face of denationalized economic processes.

It is a mistake to think that the strengthening of the European Union and international institutions necessarily presupposes a threat to democracy. It is a question of understanding that the equilibrium between national, European, and international arenas is a challenge to extend democracy to new processes. Economic and social interdependence (especially in Europe) makes some parties' decisions affect other parties in such a way that the mutualization of risks and even the intervention of other groups should be understood in the context of one's own democratic responsibility. Sovereignty, which was previously a means of configuring democratic societies, currently only serves to find decision-making arenas that unite democratic efficacy and legitimacy once it is transformed and shared. In an interdependent world, we must shift from sovereignty as control to sovereignty as responsibility (Deng, Rothchild, and Zartman 1996). From this perspective, it is worth legitimizing intervention in spaces that sovereignty wants to consider exclusive. With all the guarantees that are necessary, the same argument that has been developed to confront violence should also be advanced when it is a question of economic risks that can have catastrophic consequences on people.

How do we manage to overcome these shortfalls when democratic decisions take place in the heart of political communities that are based on confidence and solidarity as long as there is no transnational political community?

In the face of those who believe, from a rather static position, that the problem is not so much the absence of *kratos*, but rather *demos* on a global level, experience tells us that international relations can create elements of a transnational *demos* as a result of the very dynamic of international institutions or intense transactions, in terms of solidarity, confidence, and the construction of shared memories (Zürn and Waiter-Drop 2011). This is, for example, revealed by recent European history. International institutions have moved, although still in a weak fashion, from a simple aggregate of interests to communities with increasingly shared destinies. For example, the demand for unanimity has been softened to majority decisions in institutions like the International Monetary Fund or the World Bank; there are many deliberative elements of shared sovereignty in the European Union, of course, but also in the International Criminal Court, the World Trade Organization, and even, to an extent, in the United Nations Security Council.

There is no doubt that there is a conflict between the normative principles of democracy and the effectiveness of politics to resolve some particularly weighty collective problems. But international institutions are part of the solution, no matter how difficult it is, not part of the problem. Not all obligations that we have assigned to the state can actually be carried out by it with the instruments of state sovereignty. The sooner we recognize this, the sooner we will begin to think and work on a new political configuration where there is a balance between democracy, legitimacy, and functionality.

TRANSNATIONAL HUMANISM

The international community's very diverse military interventions, from Iraq to Libya, have generated intense debate. Those who highlight the contradiction of certain operations and the selective nature of those operations based on the interests of the major powers are not incorrect. It is true that intervening in other people's affairs in the name of great principles is one of the most arbitrary practices of history. The power game offers stronger states the right to decide about the sovereignty of the others. Our international relations are created out of cynicism and self-interest, something that should come as no surprise at this point.

But it is useful to remember where the responsibility for these interventions comes from. On the one hand, the reality of our interdependence has given us new responsibilities; on the other hand, we know from Rwanda or Srebrenica that strictly humanitarian treatment of crises and disasters is completely ineffective when cruel massacres and the brutal repression of the most fundamental human rights are taking place. This experience has made humanitarian discourse abandon the logic of neutrality to enter into the logic of responsibility.

While human rights have helped establish state sovereignty, nowadays they condition and question it. Various centuries of establishing the rule of law and democracy have managed to deidealize the internal sovereignty of states; it is now a question of relativizing their interests regarding foreign politics (Badie 2002). If at other points in time, human rights relativized the interior politics of states, they currently point toward international relations: the great challenge of human rights is now the discovery of humanity beyond nations. The fact is that the establishment of the state has not been accompanied by an international order in accordance with laws, as if internal security were incompatible with external norms. Taking sovereignty seriously presupposed liberating ourselves from all previous or external normative obligations; international action would end up being a pure balance of power since every state would be fully in charge of its own actions in its own territory. It is this absolute nature of sovereignty that is questioned when we formulate the responsibility for intervention against those who undermine certain fundamental values. Humanity is slowly being imposed as a point of reference for international politics, pushing back against the idea of national sovereignty or corresponding interests.

We are experiencing the breaking point of the international order: the histories of bipolarity, ideological confrontations, and rival military powers are all finished, but it is also the end of a world understood as the juxtaposition of nation-states dedicated to competing among themselves or to coexisting in mutual indifference. Globalization has made interdependence into an active principle of the international game that directly questions the very idea of sovereignty.

Sovereignty is placed into question, in the first place, because of its ineffectiveness in a context of solid interdependence. Sovereignty is overcome by the emergence of new problems that cannot be tackled alone: ecology, the growing complexity of development, the contrasts provoked by globalization, the promotion of common goods like peace, health, food, or human rights. There are fewer and fewer issues that can be managed in the strict space of the sovereign, self-sufficient state. So the logic of aggregation tends almost inevitably to trap states, out of necessity, conformity, or pressure. States—which are responsible, whether actively or passively, voluntarily or involuntarily, skeptically or acceptingly, alone or with others—end up playing the game of interdependence and entering into agreements on common goods. In this way, the idea of sovereignty is opposed to the idea of responsibility. States are ever more responsible for the world order. Once faced with a contractual responsibility to their citizens, they now also carry a responsibility that commits them to the exterior regarding goods such as the environment, peace, and development.

In its traditional form, sovereignty evokes a seriousness that should, by definition, be elevated above mistakes, doubts, and misunderstandings. It is an ultimate power from which all authority is derived, the definitive argument that is opposed to pretensions or the criticism of others, the masterpiece of the ideology that authorizes all states to become an exclusive actor on the official international stage, a centralized power that acts as the supreme authority over a territory without being answerable to anyone else.

Even though it has been unmasked, considered an ambiguous, contradictory, or maladjusted fiction, sovereignty has not been abolished. Of course, it still has a mobilizing effect and functions as an appeal to authority. What it can no longer do is establish itself as something absolute; it is one principle among others that directly contradict it. It has probably never existed in an absolute form, probably always being violated in practice by other contradictory powers. No power exists in a void without other powers capable of acting upon it, contradicting it, and modifying it. Current normalcy implies limitations on sovereignty; the state finds itself obliged to act in ways that contradict the principle that establishes it, accepting the coexistence of actors who are beyond its sovereignty. The fact is that, in the end, the state loses more sovereignty than power. Sovereignty is subjected to the corrosive effect of interdependence. But power remains, even though it is modified; the capacity for action can even increase with the cooperation that allows the sovereign state to gain access to new resources and recover its specifically political function.

In addition to the reality of interdependence, the other great limiting principle of sovereignty is respect for human rights. The violation of these rights activates the interventional community's responsibility to intervene. In the end, both principles are intertwined because what the generalized practice of intervention has precipitated is not an idealistic discovery of human rights, but the reality of our interdependence. This mutual dependence has given way to new scenarios of responsibility in which the demands for cooperation and for intervention increase: calling upon companies to invest and create employment, upon states to fulfill specific budgetary demands that do not harm society, upon international institutions to give aid or lend money, upon regional or global powers to reestablish security, and so on.

This is the context through which the United Nations formulates the principle of the "responsibility for protecting," as a responsibility that accompanies, under certain conditions, the right to intervene. Sovereignty was saved or frozen by the Cold War. Outside threats implied that the power of states remained intact, at the expense of the most serious attacks on human rights. The Eastern and Western ideological blocs thought they could ignore fundamental human requirements in the name of the principle of nonintervention. Confronted by their rivals, they employed that principle for nothing but purely rhetorical purposes. But these circumstances have changed radically. A true international politics of human rights is possible when it is no longer serving the needs of bipolar rivalry. Other people's human rights are increasingly a daily concern of international life, independent of ideological ascriptions, which no longer act as an excuse to allow intolerable situations.

International life is no longer summed up by a juxtaposition of sovereignties and a confrontation of powers. International or, better yet, transnational humanism is being forged little by little. There are already institutions capable of determining effective practices. The slow ascent of the principle of universal jurisdiction, the universalization of human rights, and the reinforcement of international integration are elements of good governance capable of tackling the dissemination of violence over the long haul.

There are many actors and networks that intervene to make the idea of humanity operative, competing with national interests and modifying the value and effectiveness of the classic resources for the exercise of power. At the same time, the reference to humanity has shifted from being a private discourse, belonging to institutions "without borders," to being politicized to the extent that states confront new responsibilities, becoming a principle of international vigilance.

Of course, we cannot yet speak about the democratization of international life: there is still a lot of arbitrary state power. It is not the case that the international politics of human rights has replaced cynicism with morality or governments with NGOs. Humanity has been evoked everywhere and at every point in time, but in the world today, this reference has a new opportunity: transnational humanism consists in placing the demand for integration beyond unilateral advantages or persuading others that these advantages are precarious if they are not inscribed into a process of international integration.

GLOBAL JUSTICE

It is relatively easy to know what we are saying when we state that someone is just or unjust; it is more complicated when we apply this description to societies or countries, even more so if we affirm that the world is unjust. This last statement, however, is frequently asserted in our daily conversations. When we make it, we are not accusing any one person specifically; instead, we are referring to a structural situation of injustice. The world is not just or unjust like a state or person can be. Appealing to a structural situation of injustice means that we are talking about properties of the world's being, which cannot be reduced to the injustice that can be attributed to concrete people, although structural injustices necessarily include the unjust actions of people.

For some people, talking about global justice is excessive; they prefer to talk about international justice, which presumes that they consider the nation-state as the correct context for justice. This primacy has dominated ideas about justice for a long time. But the dynamics of globalization have been eroding the model of international relations on the basis of some more or less independent states. For that reason, we cannot understand the consequences of climate change, the patenting of certain medications, the plundering of natural resources, the deregulation of financial markets, or hunger in the world as domestic affairs of states that are explained, justified, or managed within those state frameworks.

New realities are overpowering the approach of looking at justice within nations. I am referring to the bilevel liberal model according to which the definition and provision of justice are the responsibility of the state, while the international community should intervene in sovereign matters only in the case of serious violations of fundamental rights. The most sophisticated model in this regard is that of John Rawls who elaborates his theory of justice based on a scenario of autonomous states negotiating not global justice but foreign policy in special conferences (Rawls 1971, 1999). As his critics have pointed out, Rawls has developed a theory for the world that has broken down (Buchanan 2000). Julius (2006) wonders whether he has a current world map, and Fraser (1990) declares him inappropriate for a post-Westphalian world.

Talking about global justice—which is more radical than international justice—makes sense in an interdependent world that establishes communities beyond the state framework. One of the most banal consequences of globalization is that we are increasingly confronted with problems that affect humanity as a whole. Many problems concern us regardless of the place where we live: the means of communication and immigration bring the suffering of the world closer to us; climate change and the financial crisis have made it obvious that we live in a single world. Decisions that are adopted far from here affect us just the same. It is no exaggeration to affirm that the horizon of global experience is configuring a true "community of misery and suffering" (Höffe 1999, 20).

In this context, the theories of justice that depart from the principle that the obligations of justice are only useful for those who live in a political community or beneath a single constitution are useless. Given global dependence, the principles of justice that reign inside nations should apply on a global scale (Beitz 1979). There is also an international society where there is no political constitution, when there are, for example, communication and commerce that link human beings of the diverse areas of the world beyond national borders. Questions relating to justice do not only arise inside established legal systems. The demands for justice and the respect for human rights are also asserted in places where there are no sanctioning procedures. The obligations of justice emerge in social processes that connect people; political institutions are responses to these obligations rather than starting points (Young 2010, 329). The responsibilities of justice precede the institutions that channel them.

Questions of justice are increasingly posed on a global level, to the extent that the global level constitutes a political structure in which the vital opportunities of many human beings are decided, which permits or provokes manifest injustices. There are injustices that refer to global structures and require specific actions at that level. Let us think, for example, about the fact that commerce is regulated by a series of conventions that have positive and negative effects on diverse participants. We can illustrate this circumstance with the idea of "structural injustice," according to which Iris Marion Young (2010) refers to a complex process in which diverse actors, rules, and practices participate. To illustrate this complexity, Young proposes replacing the metaphor of structure with that of a chain, for which responsibility cannot be conceived according to the principle of causality.

The fixation on a national framework does not allow for an understanding of the nature of the poverty in the world and the corresponding structure of responsibility. Rawls, for example, saw the causes of extreme poverty only in poor countries, because of their poor government or the lack of redistribution inside these societies. But, as Pogge (1989, 2001) has noted, the fact is that the current global order is configured on the basis of incentives and regulations that contribute to these situations of poverty. Poverty is explained not only by local causes but also by factors that have to do with the international order: protectionism that impedes the opening of markets in developing countries, patent agreements that impede the introduction of generic products in those countries, and so on. We must also keep in mind that the current state of poor countries is the result of a historic process that is in many cases marked by slavery, colonialism, and genocide. In summary, their poverty and our wealth are based on a common history.

Understanding this complex but real causality is essential in order to adequately focus the debate on poverty and the actions meant to combat it. We must remove global justice from space and from "humanitarian aid," where there is a logic of donation that conceals the responsibility of the "benevolent states." We are not facing the positive obligation of reducing suffering through humanitarian aid but the negative obligation of justice that requires that we change the current order of the world in such a way that it does not continue to damage human rights.

7

CLIMATIC JUSTICE

THE atmosphere is one of humanity's common goods, and it carries a central value for life and the survival of human beings on planet Earth. The complex causes of climate change, the diverse impacts and different responsibilities of a variety of agents, the determination of what can be demanded of each individual agent place us squarely in the camp of what we could call "complex justice." It cannot be resolved with allocations according to the rules of the market but requires specific political agreements. Among the institutions that share some type of responsibility in the fight against climate change and the diverse global summits where the state of affairs is reviewed and new objectives are negotiated, a global regime of climate change is being shaped little by little. Its complexity is not and cannot be less than that which it is attempting to manage.

THE CLIMATE IS NO LONGER WHAT IT ONCE WAS

Because of climate change, we have lost meteorology as a neutral topic of conversation, an objective reference independent of our behavior, which allowed us to talk about something that affected us, but for which no one was responsible, as interesting as it was politically sterile. Anything we locate within the neutral space of fatalism is a wonderful topic for small talk, where we are looking for some common ground that is, above all, not offensive.

But the climate is no longer what it once was. With climate change, meteorology has stopped being something inevitable; one can be more or less against it, curse those who are guilty, bemoan our inability to do anything, and even be provocative by denying the evidence. Which means it is no good for creating banal consensus. This does not mean that the climate is merely a human construction or that we can do with it whatever we choose; it means that from now on, it is established as an area of responsibility (and is, therefore, inevitably controversial). One is tempted to declare that the advance of civilization means precisely that there are consistently fewer things that are unquestionable and inevitable and more for which we are responsible.

The difficulties that arise when trying to reach an agreement about how to respond to climate change stem from three relatively new characteristics of this phenomenon: its anthropogenic nature, its universality, and the density of interactions that are in play. In other words, it is a reality subject to human change, we are all affected by it, and it is not easy to understand the quantity of variables that are involved. Given this human responsibility, there is a new field of deliberation and intervention regarding what was previously an inevitable reality over which no decision had to be made. Weather and the climate, paradigms of things that are givens, are actually realities that are partially shaped by human beings and are, therefore, now the object of controversy. Our ancestors would not have understood that one can disagree with the climate and propose changing it. The climate has experienced a change in nature and appreciation similar to other realities such as health, intimacy, or inequalities: they have gone from being inevitable facts to being dependent variables and, for that reason, a topic of interest for democratic citizenry just like any other. The weather used to be, we could say, an insipid topic for elevator conversations and has now become the object of passionate debates.

If the topic is not now able to generate banal consensuses, it is due to its seriousness and complexity. Nowadays the climate is pure politics, perhaps the most serious and passionately political matter on our agenda. The period from now until 2020—a brief span of time, barely two or three legislative sessions—will determine the living conditions of upcoming generations. Climate change is without a doubt the greatest problem of collective action the world has ever had to confront. That is why one could speak of a "tragedy of commons" (Hardin 1968), and why the *Stern Review* labeled climate change as "the greatest and widest-ranging market failure" (Stern 2007).

Human beings have competed for many things throughout history, we have even killed for some of them, and now we could do so over the climate. If things continue on this path, we will face "climate conflicts" whose consequences we can barely imagine. Traditional wars over resources, regarding everything that has to do with the use of lands and access to potable water, will become more acute. Climate change will potentially also lead to conflict regarding the relationship between generations; there is obvious injustice in the fact that some people have to pay for the excesses of their ancestors or their lack of foresight and self-control.

And there will be, without a doubt, massive migrations. We can already talk about "climate refugees," in other words, people fleeing because of a climate event (Welzer 2007). This concept refers to the masses of refugees whose subsistence in their places of origin will become more difficult or impossible, in such a way that they will want to participate in the possibilities of survival of privileged countries. According to data from the Red Cross, there are currently twenty-five million such people, and it is calculated that there may be between fifty and two hundred million in 2050. We will no longer be able to distinguish between climate refugees and war refugees, because many new wars will be caused by the climate. There is a direct connection between both categories in Sudan, for example, and many indirect connections, to the extent that global warming accentuates inequalities and creates new conflicts.

The problems planted by all of this are extensive and will demand political decisions, not only market incentives. Who knows whether the politics of climate change, in addition to enriching our daily conversations, can help us carry out a renovation of politics that we knew to be necessary but that no irresistible force compelled us to undertake?

CAUSES AND IMPACTS

The governance of climate change raises, as a preliminary issue, the difficulty of identifying causes, impacts, and responsibilities in a just fashion. For each of these questions, there are similarities and differences between countries, which make them deserve responsibilities that are also differentiated.

If we begin with causes, we find great asymmetry. Global warming is caused by a plurality of actors, but the largest part of the responsibility belongs to the OECD (Organisation for Economic Co-Operation and Development) countries, because of both past emissions and their high level of emissions today.

There are ninety-some states that emit carbon dioxide at climate-changing levels because their forms of production or consumption make use of fossil fuels. It is also the case that the countries that have the greatest impact on climate change are those least affected by it, while those who barely help create it end up being the most affected. In industrialized countries, every inhabitant produces an average of 12.6 tons of carbon dioxide a year, while in the poorest countries, it is 0.9 tons. Almost half of all global emissions are due to countries that were industrialized early on, in spite of the rapid pace of emerging countries now. The *Stern Review* (2007) notes that since 1850, the United States and Europe have generated close to 70 percent of CO_2 emissions. Developed countries continue to contribute substantially to the growth of that quantity. The United States is the country with the greatest amount of CO_2 emissions (more than twenty tons per person per year); Europe and Japan, close to half of global emissions; China, a fourth; India, one-tenth; and the African continent, less than one ton per person per year. For that reason, there is huge inequality between countries when it comes to responsibility for the emission of greenhouse gases: people who live in the one hundred countries that will be most affected by climate change are only responsible for 3 percent of global emissions.

If we consider impacts, we will note that when it comes to effects, there is equality in principle, but a notable degree of inequality in reality. In the first place, climate change is a universal phenomenon, in other words, it affects everyone indistinctly, and there are no places that are absolutely protected or territorial strategies to limit its scope. Equality regarding the impacts of climate change comes from the fact that its effects are not spatially limited. Climate change ends up having a bearing on countries that are somewhat indirectly affected by it. Its consequences are not limited by the place in which it originated. States with minimal technological or economic capacity that have barely contributed to creating the problem (such as almost all the African states) as well as the countries that are most motivated to protect the climate (such as the countries in Europe) are at least as affected by its negative consequences as states with greater emissions.

But we can also prove inequitable impacts, since the effects of climate change vary depending on geographic factors. Floods will principally affect populations situated on river deltas, and the increase in sea level will affect coasts and small islands. But the principal source of inequality is poverty and different response levels based on the ability to make modifications from the infrastructural, technological, or economic point of view. Poor countries are relatively more vulnerable to damages caused by climate change (Serfati 2009). Although all countries find themselves affected by climate change, the poorest geographic areas will be the ones that suffer the greatest consequences of climate change and suffer them most intensely, since they are the ones that have the highest temperatures, as well as the most agricultural and least diversified economies. Socioeconomic factors are more significant than the climate in things related, for example, to the spread of illness. There are a thousand times more cases of dengue fever in the north of Mexico than in the south of Texas, in spite of the fact that the climate is very similar in a hundred kilometer area. The same is true of natural disasters, which affect countries in a very different manner depending on their level of development. An earthquake is not the same from one country to another, so we could probably say that, deep down, there are no natural disasters, but rather social disasters, or natural disasters whose effects are different depending on social conditions.

Climate change has very different regional effects and its social repercussions also depend on corresponding abilities. In the most advanced countries, where there is a high standard of living, good food, and a high level of protection against disasters, and in which material damages can be compensated, it is likely that the possible social consequences of climate change will be limited; regions with hunger, poverty, lack of infrastructure, and violent conflicts will be harder hit by environmental changes. Regarding these effects, there are multiple disadvantages: the same countries that will probably be most affected are those that are less able to confront those consequences. Countries that would be least affected or that could even reap benefits are more able to manage problems that might arise from any changes. The irregularity of monsoons first affects the countries in Southwest Asia, and floods threaten large river deltas, such as Bangladesh or India. Rising sea levels will be felt most on small islands, such as those in the Pacific, but also in cities such as Mogadishu, Venice, and New Orleans, which are at sea level. For rich countries like the Netherlands, it will be comparatively easier to improve their protective dikes; reforestation after a storm is better handled in Kansas than in Kerala (Santarius 2007, 19). Thus, existing global symmetries and inequalities are made more acute by climate change.

Another asymmetry that ends up further complicating matters has to do with the varying level of impact on different generations. Time is pressing, of course, but not enough to facilitate solutions, since egoistic actors can hope that they will not suffer the consequences of global warming. The demand for cooperation is weakened. For people who are alive today, solutions to this problem cost more than we would get out of them. Incentives for cooperation do not work because the generations do not coexist at the same time.

As if this asymmetrical framework were not enough, certain effects may be harmful to some groups and beneficial to others. Along with the disastrous consequences of climate change in the South (flooding, droughts, the disturbance of ocean currents, an increase in tropical diseases), there could be positive effects in the North (an increase in land values, new maritime routes) (Easterbrook 2007). Some regions will benefit since their agricultural conditions or their attractiveness to tourists could improve. Russia, for example, could benefit from future ecological crises since it has a large amount of gas and petroleum, and rising temperatures will allow for new areas of cultivation.

It is true that climate change does not affect in precisely the same way those who live in one place or another, the rich and the poor, or countries whose levels of development do or do not permit certain self-limitations. If being universally affected is a motive for reaching agreement, unequal effects mean that there are different interests that make reaching an agreement complicated. In any case, the advantages are only appreciable in the short term; by the very nature of the problem, there will eventually be only disadvantages that extend to every corner of the world. In the end, there will be nothing but losers.

The final cause of equality in the face of disaster is the fact that this "world risk society" (Beck 2007) is characterized by a degree of connectivity between diverse actors of a scope unprecedented in history (Homer-Dixon 2006, 112). This society displays the exact fulfillment of the theory of "external effects" (Swaan 1993), which says that given our high degree of interdependence, problems of poverty and health increasingly threaten every member of society, not merely those directly affected, and these problems thus require collective solutions. An awareness of this fact was at the heart of the creation of the welfare state and is just as valid today for the effects of climate change. All countries will end up being affected by it, and because of that, we need cooperative solutions. It is something Norbert Elias also noted in his sociological writings when he showed the extent to which an increase in interdependence means a decrease in power differentials between actors. He called this process a "functional democratization" (1996, 72) and it eventually ends up being institutionally manifested. Although Elias was describing this sociological mechanism on a national scale, it can also be observed nowadays at the level of global interdependence. Risks end up making the most diverse actors equal and also redirecting their varied responsibilities toward concerted actions.

A CASE OF COMPLEX JUSTICE

In addition to the complexity that stems from the analysis of causes and impacts, there is another source of complexity that stems from the global network of interdependencies that make reaching agreements on justice and government responsibilities difficult. It is not so much the number of agents involved as the complexity of the criteria of justice that appear in negotiations. Their essentially controversial character is due to the complexity of the interactions that are in play. This type of agreement puts to the test humanity's ability to reach a compromise that balances conflicting interests and distant aspirations for justice. The fact that damages are not geographically distributed with criteria of equality is not a neutral matter; there are some who lose more than others. That is why climate change has become an especially controversial political question.

In the negotiations for agreements on climate change, the climate per se is not discussed, because no one questions the need for an agreement on intervention to stop climate change. Governments seem to be in agreement about the principle of taking resolute action against the warming of the planet, but they continue to be profoundly divided about the division of efforts, fundamentally between advanced and developing countries. Controversies include the criteria of justice that will determine corresponding decisions, such as how and when responsibility is taken for the protection of the environment, by whom, and how that responsibility is divided. This does not have as much to do with the water, air, and trees as with employment and well-being. The least developed countries do not understand why they should assume the costs of the industrial nations' irresponsible development. Countries in Asia or the former Soviet bloc do not want to threaten their process of economic recuperation, while the most advanced economies resist being the ones who pay for the rest of the world. Finally, the most developed countries believe they would be unjustly affected by the restrictions. Opposing interests barely allow progress to be made on commitments.

The United Nations Framework Convention on Climate Change has been constructed on the basis of a principle of "common but differentiated responsibilities" based on the circumstances of every country (Article 4). This provision has in fact acted as an alibi for a lack of commitment to reduction on the part of developing and emerging countries, a position that has been confirmed in the Kyoto Protocol. Emerging states like China, and especially India, have not shown any disposition to renounce the advantages that have been conceded to them in this way, even though a commitment of this type should not be effected for at least ten or twenty years. At the same time, they have suspended any initiative in this direction, making it conditional on the industrialized countries, particularly the United States, demonstrating that they are going to make substantial efforts to reduce emissions.

If the commitments acquired by Europe at the Copenhagen Summit were ambitious, it is because the cost of reducing greenhouse gases is relatively lower in Europe than in other regions of the world. In economic terms, it will cost the United States as much to reduce emissions 4 percent between now and 2020 as it will cost Europeans to reduce emissions 20 percent by the same date. The comparisons of commitments regarding emission reductions cannot be fully appreciated without referencing the economic costs they entail. When Europe supports heroic environmental measures, we must keep in mind that they do so from a very favorable position.

Developing countries have presented two lines of argumentation in this regard. The first concerns the "historic responsibility" for carbon that developed economies have emitted until now. These advanced countries have used up much of the atmosphere's capacity to absorb carbon, and they should compensate developing countries for this "expropriation." It is the "development imperative" proposed by Giddens (2009, 9): the poorest nations have only contributed to global warming marginally; they must have the opportunity to develop even if this process provokes emissions, for a rather extended period. The argument is serious, but certain objections should be taken into consideration. In the first place, considering the emerging countries' desire to accelerate modernization that will allow them to recover from their historic underdevelopment, we could ask ourselves: does justice mean that everyone must have the same opportunity to destroy humanity's survival conditions? In addition, rich countries were not fully aware of the consequences; when they were developing, they believed, as almost everyone did until recently, that the atmosphere was an infinite resource. In addition, the "expropriators" are dead and buried. Their descendants, even if they could be identified, should not be considered responsible for acts they did not commit. There is a gap between cause and effect (those who create a problem and those who must resolve it are not contemporaries), which makes both the assigning of responsibility and the achievement of commitments more difficult. These objections do not completely disallow the argument of "historic responsibility" since developed economies still benefit enormously from past industrialization.

The developing countries' second line of argumentation concerns the just distribution of future carbon emissions. Let us suppose that global emissions are controlled by emission permits. Developing countries believe that these permits should be distributed on the basis of the population or per capita income. If we take population as a criterion, the reasoning is legal: every human being has the same right to use global carbon. If we focus on per capita income, the argument is egalitarian: permits should be given to the poorest populations so they can attain the same heights as the others. These two principles imply that the permits should be conceded to developing economies, whether because they represent the majority of world population or because they represent the majority of the world's poor people. The problem is that these principles are not generally recognized in international relations. If there is, for example, no agreement about the principle of dividing natural resources, why would there be agreement related to the atmosphere? Nor can we say that the idea of rigorous equalitarianism stirs great enthusiasm. Development assistance has never achieved even half of the 0.7 percent that the United Nations hoped to achieve.

To escape this labyrinth, the economists Vijay and Patel proposed applying a principle that is widely accepted as a minimal condition of impartiality: doing no harm (Vijay and Patel 2009). In the context of climate change, the application of this principle would mean allowing developing countries to reduce their efforts until they have eliminated poverty. It would be a question of allowing them to maintain their current pace of growth for some time (longer for Africa than for China, for example), after which the concession of these permits would be progressively reduced. Climate models afford us a foundation upon which we might come to an agreement on these periods of time. To accelerate the process of coming together, the transfer of certain technologies to less developed countries could be favored so they could reduce the cost of their efforts.

This approach also has the advantage of taking into consideration "historic responsibility." An important part of the damages caused by carbon accumulation in the atmosphere is the elevated costs of reduction for all countries. In the proposed model, a portion of these costs would be covered for a specific period. It also keeps the legal and egalitarian arguments in mind when conceding emission permits to the poorest countries, which is a significant financial transfer, while the distribution of permits on the basis of current emissions would benefit rich countries excessively. This transfer would only last for a certain period of time, the length of which would have to be agreed upon. This would be more acceptable for the governments and citizens of advanced countries than distributing permits based on per capita income, which would mean transferring much more to developing countries than current transfers.

Negotiations on climate change are so important that no one can allow themselves the luxury of digging in their heels.

Questions of adaptation are fundamental for successful negotiations, if we want to include countries like China, India, and Brazil in the agreements, since in the near future, they will represent a large percentage of global emissions. For this reason, distributions must be carried out in a spirit of justice. Of course, the conceptions of justice are as diverse and controversial as those of self-interest. Precisely because of this, the political skill to articulate global governance is an absolute necessity when it comes to constructing a commitment between different parties.

GLOBAL GOVERNANCE OF CLIMATE CHANGE

What type of global governance corresponds to the types of challenges raised by climate change? The heart of the difficulty could be summarized by the idea that we have trusted market solutions, and we have not made very much progress in the construction of political agreements. Why is it so necessary to make progress on agreements of a political nature in order to confront the question of climate change? Do we not already have a series of procedures that have allowed us to make a certain amount of progress? There are, of course, market solutions such as selling emissions or "joint implementation" that have led to partial results. It is also true that we will not make progress if we make decisions that fight *against* the market. The problem is that the market cannot resolve the entire issue. The market offers "appropriate signs" for the production of private goods, but not for collective goods and even less for the avoidance of "negative externalities." Market instruments are not suitable for anticipating long-term environmental costs. The economic costs of climate change are only predictable in a very approximate way. Uncertain future events are particularly resistant to precise cost assessments. This demotivates economic actors from taking these forecasts into account and makes the task for political institutions more difficult when they attempt to establish regulations that can be accepted by everyone.

It is difficult for negotiations to reach an agreement that is equal to current challenges because we benefit from the idea that behavior can be changed by economic incentives. The problem is that economic reasoning favors the attitudes of those who are called "clandestine passengers": we can presume that everyone shares in the effort, but the winner will be the one who does the least. Global public goods, more than anything else, suffer from what has been called "free riding" (Keohane 1984). The failure of negotiable emission permits is unsettling proof of this. Governmental good will does not suffice to implement a system of coercions that is imposed on everyone.

One of the consequences of neoliberal ideology has been to limit the field of possible political options, reducing the environmental economy almost exclusively to "market-based solutions," to technological innovation, and to energy efficiency (Paterson, 1996, 169). The limits of this procedure have to do with the idea that emission rights give the emitter precisely that: a "right" to continue practices harmful to the environment rather than promoting more demanding political agreements, encouraging a transformation of lifestyle and consumer habits. It is still paradoxical that the same market forces that are responsible for the problem are charged with resolving it.

Questions like climate change should be analyzed in light of another conceptual framework and managed differently. It is a question of a public good of the kind we call external to the market. We talk about external goods when the consumption or production of a good affects someone else without that being perceived by the market. As for public goods, the climate has the property of nonrivalry (everyone benefits from a stable climate), but its nonexcludability is not so evident (those who do nothing for it can benefit, at least in the short term), and to this extent, there is no market incentive to pursue it. The market, especially an energy market configured in an oligopolistic fashion, cannot produce efficient energy in the blink of an eye. All we have is the weak guarantee that climate change is perceived as a real danger for the long-term equilibrium of economies and societies. However, this warning can only be realized and addressed with political logic, concretely by policies that seriously consider the long run (Giddens 2009). That is why the climate is a good that cannot be abandoned to the market; it requires global governance.

The economic crisis has made this requirement more self-evident. We need policies more than the market, and the policies must be less prosovereignty. The world where sovereign practices made sense has changed radically in a few short decades. In order to confront climate change more efficiently, we must move toward a more cooperative world. We need a cooperative solution, a solution that is scientifically solid, economically rational, and politically pragmatic.

It is obvious that we do not have the institutions we need to manage such intense interdependence. There is no "green Leviathan" that can impose agreements and responsibilities. The international legal regime is weak; international governance on this subject is very fragmented. It is a question of a complex regime, with diverse actors, regulations, and conventions.

For those who have followed the negotiations on climate change from its beginnings, differentiation is imposed as an obvious necessity so that developing countries are progressively integrated into a binding international agreement. It was necessary during the first stage of the Kyoto Protocol for the most developed countries to be the first to move forward. Although the effects of acting unilaterally are limited, the initiative between the European Union and the United States could act as a model for other countries (Sands 2003; Aldy and Stavins 2009). In any case, the most ambitious objectives of some countries will not in and of themselves avoid global warming. Climate change demands a multinational solution.

In a situation of global competitiveness, the measures that combat climate change will not be disadvantageous to the competitiveness of the actors if everyone is required to follow them. At the same time, the difficulties of international politics in relation to climate change will not be resolved without a political effort to develop a design that promises to help and not hinder the development of Southern countries. Greenhouse Development Rights (GDR) points in this direction. If international agreements do not expressly guarantee the Southern countries' right to development, those countries could conclude that they have little to gain from policies that, in the end, restrict access to energy sources and technologies that have historically allowed growth in the developed world. GDR refers to a development threshold; countries beneath the threshold would not be prepared to assume the costs of transition since survival and development would be their priorities. In this case, they have little ability or responsibility to resolve the climate problem. That is why cooperation—which includes financial and technological transfers—is an inevitable part of the governance of climate stabilization. Even if industrialized countries reduce their emissions to something close to zero, they should also help other countries to be able to do so.

The diverse global summits that have taken place until now are a fundamental element in the construction of this complex system of governance. The objective of the Copenhagen Accord, joined by 120 countries that are responsible for four-fifths of global emissions, was the stabilization of global warming at two degrees Celsius, which constitutes progress when we remember that until that point only the European Union supported this goal. Since 2009, the G8 and G20 states have as well, but this objective is simply something countries "take note of," not a legally binding agreement in international law. It has no mechanism to guarantee that the objective is sustained. The problem with these agreements is that they result in obligations that states impose on themselves, so there is no way they can be sanctioned for failing to comply.

Climate change is a typical phenomenon of "glocalization," of interdependence between local actions and omissions with global effects. This problem is, in a way, the prototype of the complex scenarios that exist in a globalized world: there are no actions that have consequences only on the local level, nor is there any transnational institution that can manage these issues from a global perspective. The way we solve this question will be a model for the solution to similar conflicts. It is clearly a question of managing complexity: complexity of responsibilities, of potential impacts, of the costs of action, as well as the strategic performances the states develop out of the diverse questions that are in play.

8

A POLITICS OF HUMANITY

REALITY has been *communist* for a few years now. The Cold War was won by capitalism, but current events are imposing problems that place care for the *communal* rather than care for the individual at the center of our concerns. Globalization is often associated with privatization (with economic liberalization or the movement of certain goods and services toward the marketplace), but it can also be understood as an increase in what is public, the fact that societies are more interdependent. The political agenda is now full of common problems, of universal public goods. I am not talking about a battle of ideas but of actual combat, of realities that push their way forward against the inertia of isolated and immediate interests.

Public goods are one of the most fundamental problems of our societies today, and we know that the strategies used to confront them must also be common. Problems like environmental pollution, climate change, and the exploitation of natural resources, financial integration and the risks associated with it, global inequality, and the population explosion, global crime that is manifested in drug and weapon trafficking, these are all questions that have become part of the political agenda. Increased integration of the global economy accentuates them and modifies the context in which they must be handled. Complex global systems, ranging from the financial to the ecological, connect the fate of local and distant communities. One's own security dissolves into general security: everyone depends on everyone else, the security of any one person is in direct proportion to the security of others, whether they are nearby or far away. We are increasingly interested in what happens to other people because we believe that will help us identify possibilities and threats for ourselves as well. We already have concrete experience in the areas of security, the economy, and the environment that prove the clumsiness of only pursuing things for ourselves; these experiences suggest the need to learn to make use of cooperative intelligence. *Common* sense is imposed, which is more political discovery than epistemological category: once we realize how intermingled our self-interest is with other people's interests, we see how important it is to understand these connections as soon as possible.

The logic of interdependence presents new difficulties for nation-states, modifying our goods and our public spaces. This points toward the goal of a politics of humanity. In other words, it suggests that humanity as a whole (whatever that may be) can act as a whole and that we must configure a level of governance that corresponds with the nature of universal common goods that are asserted with increasing insistence in the delimited spaces of globalization.

NEW INTERDEPENDENT PUBLIC GOODS

When the first theories about globalization were formulated a few years ago, some authors tried to minimize the novelty of that phenomenon by signaling that other moments of recent history had been characterized by strong internationalization and economic integration. The argument arose from comparing our current situation with the period from 1870 to 1913, the "golden age of the international economy." It is an observation that contains its share of truth, but it overlooks the protectionism of the age and the fact that business flowed through colonial channels and was, therefore, not at all similar to our reticulated reality. It also fails to keep in mind that economic integration at that time was organized in a vertical fashion, with simple, hierarchical connections, between sovereign states, without any international institutional framework. At that moment in history, it was possible to have close involvement between nations and even reciprocal causal relationships, but there was not, strictly speaking, interdependence in the sense we understand it today.

The most telling indicator of the fact that we find ourselves in another reality nowadays is the radicalness with which the logic of interdependence situates us in the face of common public goods of humanity and the global risks to which we are equally vulnerable. Public goods are those goods whose benefits—or costs, in the case of public bads—potentially affect all people, countries, and even generations. The clearest case is the global environment, but there are others such as knowledge, health, peace and security, financial stability, market efficiency, the conservation of biodiversity, and access to water. This is the ambiguous logic of interdependence: trade and financial flows make economic crises have widespread effects, even upon the most robust economies. For example, lax criteria when it comes to food security can create problems in other parts of the world because of tourism and exportation; ease of communications also facilitates tax evasion, money laundering, and drug trafficking. For public goods, the principle defined as "the triangle of publicness" is valid: consumption, benefits, and decision-making procedures must be public (Kaul et al. 2003).

Large political affairs have been almost completely dissociated from the defining framework of the states in three ways: by the creation of the problem (who or what type of behavior causes a particular problem), the impact of the problem (who suffers what type of negative effects), and the solution to the problem (who is responsible for its resolution and in what way) (Mayntz 2009, 74). The origin, the impact, and the solution of certain problems (problem generation, problem impact, problem coping) do not coincide with the limits of traditional unity as represented by societies that are organized in states. All of it defines a framework of interdependence or mutual dependency that implies shared vulnerability.

To understand this new situation, we need to understand the implications of the modern nation-state and current challenges that are demanding a profound transformation of it. The success of the modern political system—which is usually said to have begun with the Peace of Westphalia (1648)—is attributed to two conquests that mutually reinforced each other. In the first place, there is the ability of states considered individually—their endogenous structures, processes, and institutions—to effectively organize public space and provide public goods *in the domestic sphere*, at the same time as they neutralize exterior interferences and protect society from what economists call "exogenous shocks." The second conquest is the ability of states *in the plural* to develop a system of rules, norms, and practices that limit or regulate direct conflict between them and reinforce a series of lasting common resolutions that arise out of their inevitable interaction (treaties, business agreements, monetary systems, and the like). Because of these two abilities, states have been in the position to organize internally and to temper the inevitable external "anarchy" that is derived from their sovereignty.

Both abilities are, then, made more fragile by globalization: states are not in any condition to guarantee the internal public goods that they promised, and the mere juxtaposition of sovereign states is not enough to guarantee external public goods. In the face of both objectives, we are all failed, insufficient states. The states and the system of sovereign states have serious difficulties when it comes to promoting stability, security, prosperity, and other specifically collective goods. States can no longer guarantee many public goods that they used to provide since they have been shaped transnationally or are supplied by the markets.

We are now modifying the idea we had about public goods, which were until recently connected with state sovereignty, which was responsible for guaranteeing them. We are slowly becoming more conscientious that these goods are not divisible between states. For example, the environment, security, economic stability, and symbolic goods (essentially human rights) cannot be managed sovereignly without causing serious negative consequences. Global crises or global risks affect not only the most directly concerned national communities, but the whole of humanity, because of the chain of consequences or side effects. To the extent that they are common goods of humanity, public goods stop being only sovereign goods. International conferences on some of these matters are proof that we are conscious that their management surpasses the abilities of sovereign states. Even regarding the states' principal abilities, like defense and security, states find themselves challenged as the legitimate provider of those collective goods. At the same time, the power to establish and maintain the global order has been fragmented or is shared by the states.

From the point of view of what we can accurately denominate "the common public goods of humanity," sovereignty is not in any condition to resolve the principal problems that affect us. An isolated, unilateral political stance makes no sense for the majority of these problems. Fundamental decisions are no longer adopted at the national level, where the only decisions being made are frequently on incidentals. On commercial, monetary, fiscal, or social matters, decisions have become profoundly interdependent, which establishes a way of governance that implies not only a reinforcing of intergovernmental coordination, but also the creation of mobilizing spaces and the representation of interests, of discussion, and of public debate that transcend national territories and sovereign ways of thinking.

In this manner, the principle of responsibility is imposed on the principle of autonomy. The states are forced to recover spaces of action in exchange for agreeing to enter into the game of shared power. Vulnerability in the face of new risks is not something that modifies only legal sovereignty, but also operational sovereignty, in other words, the capacity of the states to assert themselves in ordinary political affairs (Reinicke 1998, 56). Although principles and declarations are maintained through traditional inertia, the reality is that states have long since exchanged sovereignty for power.

Mutual exposure to global risks regarding security, food, health care, finances, or the environment reinforces our interconnection and contributes to the configuration of humanity as a new subject that is constituted not on a metaphysical level, but on the fact of interdependence. Thinking about ourselves as one unique humanity has nothing to do nowadays with a monistic and authoritarian totality; we live in a united but not singular world, interrelated but not homogenized. It is a question of thinking about common existence without falling into global indifference or the universalization of the local community (Pulcini 2009, 277; Cerruti 2007, 169). A politics of humanity should not presume a transposition of old monisms on a global scale, but the opportunity to think of the political subject with inclusive but not totalizing categories.

THE GOVERNANCE OF GLOBAL CAPITALISM

The relationship between markets and politics is especially problematic since capitalism has been converted into a global force devoid of the moderating powers of the nation-state. If governing the economy has never been an easy task, global capitalism seems to be literally ungovernable, beyond our control.

Globalization is making the task of governing the markets more difficult, in the first place, because it has created a fundamental inconsistency between, on the one hand, the global reach of economic and financial transactions and, on the other, the local reach of rules and regulations, which exposes nation-states to management incompetence for global crises. The capabilities of the nation-state have been limited while necessary capabilities have not been transferred to global institutions. The disparity between globalized markets and national political systems is a challenge for the global political economy. The governing of capitalism will be impossible as long as the instruments of governance remain limited to nation-states and their fragmented and easily circumvented supervisory capabilities.

The second reason is the opacity of the financial system and its complicated formulations that escape state control, making supervision and responsibility difficult. We are immersed in a network of nontransparent risks through credit instruments and a massive system of shadow banking that conceals transactions, protects the lack of transparency, and covers with a veil of ignorance a large portion of the financial system operating beyond banking supervision and national regulation. All of this has made global capitalism into an economic system that is very prone to crisis, with a level of instability and uncertainty that has no precedents in human history. It is extraordinarily vulnerable to systemic risk (Roubini and Mihn 2011, 210).

The challenge presented by the two-pronged reality of deterritorialization and a lack of transparency is huge. We must conceptualize economic policies articulated by a model of governance for very complex systems, with highly dense interactions and elevated technological sophistication. The first thing that is required is a good analysis of the interaction between economics and politics and a good diagnostic of the current economic crisis.

We need to confront, from the beginning, a paradox that has left us perplexed and that explains the current powerlessness of governments. We could, without worrying about the details that will need to be filled in later, say: the market has failed, but that has not led to a strengthening of the states. How do we explain this situation and the consequences it has for what we should do in the future?

The financial crisis has destroyed the myth of freely self-regulating markets. The market cannot produce its own preconditions—for example, the rule of law, the institution of private property, or the prevention of monopolies—and for that reason, it needs the regulatory power of politics. This need is even more urgent at a time when globalization has increased market instability, especially the volatility of the financial markets. In this context, there are possibilities and spaces for the governing of the marketplace that, although they are limited, would allow the political system to safeguard its long-term interests both from society and from the economy. Markets depend on an institutional framework and this is where politics can act: making economic transactions easier or more difficult according to institutionally designed political objectives.

However, the collapse of the markets does not imply a neo-Keynesian return of the state. The global economic crisis smashed the budgets that believed in the self-regulatory stability of the markets, but it has not confirmed the superiority of politics or the state (since they have been unable to limit credit, regulate financial innovations, limit public debt, or prevent the opacity of the banking system). The states are not in a strong position regarding the decisions they should make in order to escape the crisis. The states' ability to govern is ever more subject to international dependence and global constrictions regarding what has come to be called "disaggregated sovereignty" (Slaughter 2004, 266): the spread of power in a multilevel political construction, with states that have lost power and many of their prerogatives (especially regulatory authority), in the midst of powerful flows and transnational networks. Sovereignty is no longer an absolute category but a concept that designates the abilities that are available in a context of mutual dependence.

The efforts of democratic societies to control markets and externalities by intervening directly in the economy have been of very little use. The lesson we must draw from this experience is that the political governance of capitalism is more complicated and should be more indirect in order to establish a balance between the autonomy of the economic system and the framework of political orientation. While Adam Smith famously demanded that states provide "peace, easy taxes and a tolerable administration of justice," the demands are now more complex and sophisticated. The sooner we abandon the tone of moralizing simplicity that is searching for responsible parties and calling for a generic change of values, the sooner we will address the task of understanding and governing an especially complex reality.

If we can take any lesson from the current state of the crisis, it is that neither the market alone nor isolated state authority is capable of establishing the type of complex regulatory framework necessary to confront the opacity, volatility, and uncertainty that characterize the functioning of global finances. This means that the governing of the markets should not be understood as a simple strengthening of governments in the face of markets. The global financial system is too important and has too many consequences for it to be abandoned to the control of private organizations, and too complex and sophisticated to be managed by public institutions. For that reason, the goal consists in configuring a mixed system of governance that includes components of self-organization and public supervision. We must have a hybrid method of exercising authority in those cases in which neither public nor private authorities can go it alone because, fundamentally, public authorities lack knowledge and private authorities lack power.

Authoritative modes of governing are not very effective in the global marketplace. Although it is true that we should improve the power of global institutions, we should not forget that many of the components of governance are not an exercise of power, but a group of incentives that are realized through rational argument, the expectation of mutual benefit, or the fear of damaging reputations. That is why, in addition to regulatory institutions with regional or global scope, it is very important to have "watch-dog" entities like Transparency International, consumer organizations, and diverse social movements that observe matters globally. We talk about the global governance of capitalism precisely to refer to a complex system in which there are elements of self-regulation, global institutions, state authority, procedures for cooperation, and informal regulations that come from international business or global monitoring associations.

I would like to summarize these possibilities of market governance into five tasks on which politics can take the lead: (1) improve regulations; (2) work on systemic risks; (3) strengthen cognitive capacities; (4) institutionalize the protection of the future; and (5) guarantee social coherence.

(1) In the first place, it is a question of understanding that we are faced with a problem not of *more* regulation but of *better* regulation. Market function can be just as undermined by excess as by a lack of liberty, by too much or too little regulation. In the current globalized world, what most weakens the market is *inadequate* regulation. Poor regulation can have negative effects, as has been the case with the establishment of shadow banking systems or procyclical dynamics.

It does not make any sense for us to once again put into place a new cycle of regulation and deregulation; the global, financialized economy of the knowledge society requires a new approach. There is no guarantee that regulation will prevent future crises when we fail to understand their function and improve their governance, by making use of innovative procedures rather than the kind of thinking that makes us oscillate between deregulation and control.

(2) The principal source of the renovation of global economic governance comes from *paying attention to systemic risks*. The most important challenge that contemporary society has when it comes to governing markets is the management of systemic

risks. This is a responsibility that cannot be left in the hands of economists and financial actors; it is a task for the political economy and the theory of governance. In an interconnected world, there is an increase in unintended systemic effects. The financial crisis has made it dramatically apparent that the growing global interdependence of a great number of actors can result in adverse systemic effects. The evolution of the crisis, its potential for economic self-destruction, and the perplexity of experts have substantiated the ideas of those who have interpreted it as a crisis caused by systemic ignorance, not asymmetrical information (Skidelsky 2009). Systemic risks call on public interest and political responsibility to establish regulatory provisions capable of preventing them. In questions of systemic gravity (financial matters, environmental affairs, pandemics, the proliferation of nuclear weapons, and so on), private self-government is important but insufficient to handle such risks.

A systemic risk is a risk of vicious circles that destabilize interconnected markets. Systemic risks arise from an opaque interaction between "layered and leveraged components of a concatenated compound" (Willke and Willke 2012, 35). We find ourselves here in a maze of broad side effects belonging to a new capitalism that is characterized by the complex interplay of components, which gives rise to unexpected combinatory effects.

The attention to systemic issues presupposes a radical makeover of our point of view and our governmental procedures, which are shortsighted about everything that is not immediate and concrete. We should be concerned about this catastrophic linking, not about the bad intentions of individuals as much as the fatal interactions of the system. When regulatory focus is placed exclusively on singular actors, governance becomes blind to systemic turbulence. Of course, this turbulence has its origin in particular actions, but these actions become avalanches when a series of chain reactions is placed in motion within a financial system that is not designed to prevent them. This altered point of view is what the United States Treasury Department invoked after the crisis broke out: "regulators did not take into account the harm that large, interconnected, and highly leveraged institutions could inflict on the financial system" (U. S. Treasury 2009, 5).

(3) Governments should *improve cognitive capacity* and evolve toward a form of political decision-making based on knowledge. Good governance depends on decisions being supported by expert knowledge and legitimated democratically. In a knowledge society, there is greater demand that decisions are based on knowledge, in other words, more on cognitive considerations than on value judgments, which does not mean that politics must sacrifice its function in the face of experts but that politics itself must adopt a style that is more cognitive than normative.

Financial transactions, models, and derivatives have become very sophisticated, and their consequences are difficult to anticipate. If regulators do not understand them, then they certainly cannot regulate them. In fact, regulating institutions are continuously soliciting the advice of the best risk professionals. Regulatory authority will only be the result of collaboration and not the exclusive and stable recourse of governments.

Timothy Geithner, former Secretary of the Treasury for the Obama administration, said in 2008: "We need to build a system that is safe against uncertainty, against ignorance, against the failure to identify the future source of crisis" (2008, 5). However, the true epistemological revolution that the current economic crisis demands is, instead, abandoning the assumption of exactitude and the recognition that governing is managing ignorance, assuming the uncertainty that comes from governing complex systems.

There is an element of inevitable opacity in contemporary capitalism that has to do with emerging phenomena or hard-to-foresee systemic results. Paradoxically, it is less difficult to recognize this ignorance than to be ostentatious about certainty. "Nothing undermines openness more surely than certainty. Once we feel as if we have 'the answer,' all motivation to question our thinking disappears. But the discipline of systems thinking shows that there simply is 'no right answer' when dealing with complexity" (Senge 1990, 281). Previous (and some current) errors related to the economic crisis show exactly how this inclination to not consider the ignorance that accompanies financial risks affects particular risk strategies and interaction between various sectors of the financial system.

(4) Governments should be long-term protectors who are in charge of *institutionalizing the protection of the future* through foresight, responsibility, precaution, and sustainability.

In many aspects, contemporary society depends on the ability of its actors and systems to go beyond the perspective of the short term and commit to medium- and long-term projects. The shortsightedness of the financial strategies that made certain technologies possible has endangered other values that are very important for the economy, such as the stability of currency. The experience of the crisis encourages us to modify our relationship with time and with various types of decisions. It would be a question of transforming myopic short-term rationalities into viable futures, acting strategically instead of responding to immediate demands or reacting to short-term necessities.

(5) One of politics' essential roles is the *promotion of the coherence of the social whole*, especially when we are within a form of capitalism that has lost its sense of belonging to society, its place in a social context, and its obligations toward society.

The ability of markets to govern themselves is fundamental to the distributed intelligence that characterizes modern and functionally differentiated societies by virtue of their professional expertise, specialized knowledge, and technological instruments. Social subsystems need this autonomy since there is no central summit or hierarchy capable of controlling everything. However, this self-governing has some limits, particularly the limits that derive from market failures and excessive negative externalities such as, for example, the incongruence between strategies of maximization in the short term and sustainability in the long term (Stiglitz 2010, 15). In differentiated societies, social subsystems are very specialized and concerned only with their own matters (the economy, science, health, and culture), which creates problems of integration and general coordination. There is a proliferation of heterogeneous logics (profitability, truth, assistance, innovation, and so on), which sometimes puts social coherence at risk. This is where politics has the inescapable responsibility to coordinate and integrate.

When certain actions can have cumulative effects or present systemic risks, then it is a question of something sufficiently relevant in social terms so that it is not abandoned to private responsibility, whether by people or by organizations. These are the limits, in my judgment, of trusting everything to corporate social responsibility, no matter how important that may be. If it is a question of "social" responsibility, its definition inevitably constitutes a formative act of political will.

The conclusion we can reach from all this is that the double challenge for the global governance of capitalism consists in bridging the gap between territorial regulatory institutions and global economic groups, on the one hand, and the gap that still exists between traditional bureaucratic modes of organizing regulation and the necessity of configuring highly sophisticated and expert models and regulatory processes, on the other.

GOVERNING DELIMITED SPACES

Conflicts and disasters are highly inconvenient, but have at least some positive features. They have an integrative approach because they reveal that there is no choice but to find global solutions, something that is not possible without perspective, institutions, and global norms. What is occurring is, in fact, an involuntary politicization of the risk society, because risks, when they are well understood, pressure societies toward cooperation. Disasters challenge limits, national agendas, and the self-sufficiency of systems; they distort priorities and force enemies to establish alliances. Threatened common spaces mean space for action, coordination, and common responsibility. This often leads to the discovery that unilateral strategies are excessively expensive and that cooperation presents solutions that are more efficient and long lasting. Cooperation modifies the perception of risks, reduces uncertainty, and affords information to the actors.

In this regard, we need to develop a whole new cosmopolitan understanding of common goods, sharpening our sensibility toward the effects of interdependence and thinking in terms of a public good that cannot be managed alone, but requires multilateral coordinated action. The true emergency of our time is to civilize globalization or make it cosmopolitan, carrying out a true "politics of humanity." Creating a politics of humanity means configuring strategies to reflexively self-limit social agents to benefit their own interests. From the cultural point of view, it means getting civilizations and cultures to understand the dependency that connects them to other cultures for their self-definition and the enrichment that the processes of transfer, exchange, and hybridization presume. From the political point of view, it implies the search for a new way of articulating public interest in an area whose scale and significance we barely recognize.

Within this panorama, although many people continue to believe that governments are the central actors in world politics, there is a growing consciousness that the functions of governance are exercised through a variety of institutional forms and, in certain contexts, governments are not necessarily the most important actors (Held and McGrew 2002). At the same time, the reality confronting states is being radically transformed. The traditional conception that viewed states as unitary, egotistical actors that coexist in an anarchic environment corresponds with the "realistic" theory of international relations, according to which the interests of states are predetermined. Given this conception, states are only capable of conceiving their inclusion in globalization as part of a zero-sum game, conflictive by definition, and only acceptable in a strictly interstate framework. But both aspects—the autarchy and the predetermination of its interests—are intimately connected and have been placed into question from the moment when the interdependence of the problems they need to resolve has become more evident.

It has been revealed that the state by itself (even the most powerful one) does not have the critical dimension in the age of globalization. It is a question of abandoning the idea of negative sovereignty (the absence of external interference) in favor of the positive sovereignty that prepares states to act and collaborate both domestically and internationally (Jackson 1990, 26). The current idea of international competitiveness between states is incompatible with the treatment of global problems, and for that reason, we should advance toward a cooperative model. It is a profound paradigm shift since we are accustomed to thinking within a multipolar world, in other words, a world of noncooperative rules of force. Perhaps the idea of interdependence, as a substitute for or corrector to sovereignty, leads to discovering all of humanity in peoples and buying into the idea that some practices more than others facilitate the development of common goods. Today we are more conscious that the price of convergence diminishes and the price of solitary conduct tends to rise. At the same time, it is increasingly difficult for the pursuit of one's own interests to not also imply benefits for others.

These circumstances are demanding something more than the mere juxtaposition of state interests. They point to global governance or, to put it another way, a politics of humanity. The label "international community" covers a partially realized reality in an ambiguous way: international conventions, the progress of multilateralism, the profusion of organisms with a global reach. The imperfect structure of international institutions is also evident. Some of them have a solid center where decisions are made while other states remain on the margin. What we really have, then, is incomplete integration into a world that unites in technological, economical areas and even in certain products and cultural styles. This same world reveals itself to be particularly illiterate when it comes to its political and legal articulation. Contrary to the expectations of the neofunctionalists and others, economic integration has not generated a parallel process in the political arena. The demand for global governance is growing because of increasing interdependence in the economic, military, and environmental realms. These new circumstances demand that we give a true political dimension to the cosmopolitanization that actually exists, which is made up of domination and unilateralism.

We currently find ourselves in a political void to some extent, where the state, as a traditional place of order and government, is not capable of confronting some of the fundamental problems it is facing, while the global framework of governance is weak. Delmas-Marty (2010) affirms that we are living at a historic point in time in which sovereignty is overrun and pluralism is contested. At the same time, the value of public goods cannot be effectively established by markets and requires particular collective decisions as well as certain regulatory frameworks. Given the increasing interdependence of problems, there is an ever-growing demand for elaborating transnational forms of regulation. A transition is being produced that is moving us from classic forms of intergovernmental cooperation to international institutions that are more intrusive in national spaces and that, for that reason, require new forms of legitimation.

However, global governance does not consist in a hierarchical management structure. The process of global governance is not the imposition of one level over another but the articulation, often fragile and conflictive, of diverse levels of governance. We are not about to create an inclusive system in which global decisions are adopted, nor, in view of the complexity of the problems at hand, does that seem desirable. In place of a "worldocracy" that coordinates the distinct tasks that belong to an integrative process, there will be multiple regional institutions that act autonomously to resolve common problems and produce different public goods (Schmitter 1999). We will not have a world government but a system of governance formed by institutionalized regulatory agreements and procedures that demand certain behaviors without written constitutions or constitutions that wield hard power. This is the sense in which governance can be defined as the ability to do certain things without the ability to order them, in other words, a type of authority, rather than jurisdiction (Rosenau and Czempiel 1992, 250). "What prepares an actor to obtain other actors' agreement in a disintegrating world is an interdependent convergence of necessities rather than a constitutional requirement that assigns supreme authority exclusively to states and national governments" (Rosenau 1999, 297). The result of all this is more of a destructuralized battleground than a formal negotiation. There is a possibility for participatory intervention, but there could also be some kinds of pressure or hegemony.

Some people have looked skeptically at the possibilities of globalizing the law, solidarity, or politics, calling attention to the political difficulties of these goals. Avishai Margalit, for example, wonders what electorate could achieve these goals since "the cosmos has no politics," lacks a political body, does not vote or decide (Margalit 2009). In contrast to that observation, we can be assured, in the first place, that the difficulties of politics in the domestic sphere are just as challenging; there are many problems of governability there too. The politics of humanity need not be more difficult than, for example, the politics of national citizens, when these communities were not yet constituted or now that societies are more fragmented. There is, additionally, an objection in principle against thinking that politics cannot be carried out on a different and unprecedented sphere from previously constituted spaces. Certainly, the majority of political problems have not had, at the time of their emergence, either the subject or the procedure needed for their resolution. Politics always has a "constituent" dimension; the decision-making subject is constituted when the problem arises and not the other way around. There is even the possibility of a democracy without *demos*, as is the case with the current European experiment.

It is not true that the processes of interdependence lead to an extinction of politics (also understood as the end of ideologies or even the end of history), as is celebrated from the neoliberal point of view or bemoaned from the point of view of classic sovereignty. Quite the opposite, in fact. If politics is the articulation of forms of coexistence on the global plane, we have the task of political reinvention similar to the invention of political communities throughout history. It is a question now of how we should coexist, how to organize ourselves, and what our reciprocal obligations are in the context of the profound interdependence generated by globalization. In that way, globalization does not have any reason it must necessarily be a process of depoliticization. Those who think that way do not understand that current challenges consist in extending democracy beyond the nation-state. Democratization within our societies should be extended to delimited spaces and transnational processes. We have the opportunity and the challenge of disconnecting political legitimacy from its connection to limited spaces.

Globalization presents many restrictions for politics, but it does not mean its end and may mean the beginning of a new era for politics. As Beck (2002, 364) says, it is not that politics has died, but that it has emigrated from classic delimited national spaces to interdependent global scenarios. Although the regimen of global governance is not directed by the mode of politics belonging to nation-states, politics has a genuine task both for the structural elaboration of that regimen and for the configuration of corresponding decision-making processes.

EPILOGUE

Us and Them

In a world like ours that belongs to everyone and to no one, a world of shared threats and common goods, where ownership should be reexamined, and demands for cooperation are stronger and stronger, a world that opens and protects itself, in which we are all equally exposed and which lacks outskirts, wrapped in interdependence and contagions, the most difficult and at the same time most demanding questions are: Who are we? How should we who live in this common world conceive of ourselves and how should we act? Making the distinction between us and them is crucial to determining our duties, our rights, and our responsibilities.

It would be wise to begin by recognizing that these are difficult questions and do not depend on assumed evidence, as if there were no distinction between us and ourselves. A preconception of this type is hidden in no small number of the ways in which we understand collective identity, in the elitism of the experts, in certain self-protective reflexes, in solidarities that conceal exclusions, but also in some of the animosity that emerges against representation and intermediation under the flag of direct democracy or economic self-regulation. These are examples of some ways of thinking and acting that assume the answer to the question about who we are.

Human beings have a tendency to stop seeing the contingency of collective groupings. Throughout history, we have divided the first-person plural in various ways: those of us who belong to the same class, laugh at the same things, are united by fear, patriots, cosmopolites, revolutionaries, those who are civilized, fellow citizens, the people, those who share the same values or the same self-interest, those who are living at the same time, our side, our generation, those who share our cause, those who are from here, the same old gang, the victims of a tragedy or an injustice, those who are irritated or threatened, experts, men, those of us who are right or normal, orthodox or sane, those who trust or fear one another, and so on. All of humanity's conquests have been preceded by an interrogation about these obvious groupings that generally conceal operations of exclusion. What would happen if we were not exactly the ones we are?

It is increasingly complicated to establish exactly who we are and who they are. The word "us" does not name a reality, but a problem (Garcés 2011, 105). Asking ourselves who we are is now a way of unsettling that first-person plural that tends to obscure its contingency. Any ethical or political reflection should begin by unsettling those who present these facts in order to question whether we are so many or so few, the reasons for belonging or disaffection, how borders with others are fixed, how the passing of time influences those boundaries, the types of transactions that should be established between what is ours and what is theirs, the difference between delegating and being estranged, the conditions of representation. Because these troublesome types of questions—who are we? why are they not part of us?—are the ones that will allow us to distinguish a genuine group from one that is shameful, a subject of responsibilities and rights in the face of an alienated crowd.

I am talking about the contingency of the "us" in all its various manifestations because it is not a question of subverting a stable value and transforming it into its contrary—as many are capable of doing, with unquestionable theoretical usefulness, from ideologies of suspicion to deconstruction. We are capable of showing, as Luhmann noted ironically, that "this is in fact that" and establishing with the same evidence a new category by inverting what had been dominant: heterodoxies, infrastructure, prisons, that which is concrete and the exception, proximity, the postcolonial, the deviation, and so on. The evidence that we snatched from the traditional "us" does not correspond to the others either. Contingency, in relation to the subject that concerns us, means that the category of "us" continues to be useful and truthful but is at the same time variable, contextual, and in need of revision.

The totality is now only thinkable as "polemic totality" (Röttgers 1983). In the face of categorical hegemonies such as the nation-state, Western civilization, or delimited spaces, the current multiplication of contexts (visible in phenomena such as interdependence, shared risks, and the intensification of mobility and communication) confers a vague fluidity on social reality. There is the creation of a complexity that affects what Luhmann (1981, 195) has called "primordial experiences of difference," dualities such as close/far, mine/theirs, familiar/strange, friend/enemy. These experiences that oriented us now require redefinition, which particularly affects the distinction between us and them.

My entire philosophical trajectory has been a reflection on intersubjectivity, on the communal. The perspective that has interested me is what we could call decentralized intersubjectivity: hospitality, contingency, dissent, difference, invisibility, estrangement, cognitive dissonance, risk. These are categories that, rather than helping us toward a triumphant consolidation of the us, help us question and contextualize it. I think that the problem of the us is not resolved from the perspective of an epistemology of intersubjectivity, as transcendental philosophy and its derivations have tried, but in a sociopolitical vein, if we manage to devise something that is truly communal. I hope to address this question by separating the sociocultural priority of the communal from the methodological priority of a philosophy of subjectivity. We are "us" because there is something that constitutes us as such when it affects us, for which we are responsible, because we protect ourselves, we share the same fear, we are equally threatened, and so on. A perspective of this type would allow us to overcome the paradigm of consensus and contract in order to think about the "us" as a result of what is in play.

I will develop this idea with minor modifications to Kant's well-known thinking about what we are (the ontology of the us), what we can know (the epistemology of the us), what we should do (the practices of the us), and what we have the right to expect (the convergence of the us). I will summarize the configurations of the us in eleven forms.

ONTOLOGY OF THE US

The Identity That Constitutes Us

Every time we reflexively examine the concept of the us, it seems less comprehensible and more contingent. This contingency of our identity is manifested on two planes, which we could call static and dynamic.

Statically, our identity cannot be conceived based on exclusivist and closed ideas, from which we construct stereotypes that delimit strangers, among other things. Because what is ours is also constituted and enriched by the continuous encounter with the unknown. In the same way that we have learned that the tradition every group appeals to is often a product of nostalgia, of selection, and of dramatization, in other words, something that comes quite close to falsification, collective identities are also the result of a social construction. Identities have frequently been constructed through interior homogenization and the exile of the unknown. In the best-case scenario, belonging and delimitation in the face of the Other allowed tolerance of interior otherness as special cases, as minorities. Of course there was diversity, but it was organized around a dominant or hegemonic identity. This approach has hindered the development of an ability to organize coexistence in a single space of that which belongs to us and that which belongs to others.

What most contributes to making identities flexible is the consciousness that the distinction between us and them is a contingent, mobile construction with porous margins. It is a discovery that contradicts our natural tendency to create a choreography of self-confirmation for ourselves. The mere fact of establishing the lack of evidence for any "us" implies a criticism of the ways of thinking that reduce things to uniformity, homogeneity, and consensus. The vocabulary of description and cultural analysis must be expanded to include space for irregularity, exception, and disagreement. Culture does not represent a closed unit, something fundamentally ours, which was only confronting the danger of becoming blurred on its margins by modernization and immigration. A cultural system is an open, mobile reality, whose vitality depends on knowing how to manage internal plurality and to dialogue with external estrangement.

The subjugation of otherness is not an inescapable destiny; dealing with something unknown can be learned. Xenophobia is not an inevitable constriction of nature. Human beings are capable of breaking the tautological identity and putting into play the ability to have relationships, giving form to authenticity in expressions that can be recognized by others. Maturity, in the personal and social realm, could be understood as the realization of one's own particularity, the discovery that our ways of understanding the world or acting upon it are contingent and, from some perspectives or for some people, strange and even ridiculous.

Derrida's (1993) "spectrology" presented this contingency of the us in a very original fashion. In the face of triumphant identity, the presence of "ghosts," in other words, of something that destabilizes our present, places in question the obviousness of the separations between us and them, alive and dead, present and absent. The ghost is what prevents the present—unity, identity—from closing in on itself; it is the sign of that opening, the place in which the nonpresent appears, the otherness that is housed in the present and questions its sovereignty. Within that instability, there is, according to Derrida, promise and hope regarding what can arrive without having been projected. It is not a question of the possibility, obviously uncertain and not guaranteed, of a realizable plenitude—as Bloch seems to think—but the impediment that a similar order presents itself as absolute, forming a whole, camouflaging that which does not fit, closing any openness to the question with its answers. This hope is not the overcoming of death and the triumph of life, but the experience of a life touched by death.

This is the only conception of the us that strikes me as legitimate: the conception of an us that is never full and in control of itself, always exposed to the visitor, undermined by otherness, inhabited by guests. Recognizing this "imperfection" that constitutes us is the only way to prevent the us from becoming totalized in exclusive complacency.

The Stories That We Are

The other aspect of the contingency of the us that I would like to address is rather dynamic. This is the question of how we have become what we are. Also from this temporal perspective, our "natural" tendency leads us to ignore the lack of historical necessity for the us that we have become. Contingency here means that our identity is not logical or nomological or intentional, but is instead the result of an exception or particularization. To say it bluntly: we are what we are because we did not manage to become what we hoped. This is what Paul Valéry was suggesting when he complained that it is impossible to do anything without everything becoming involved. The identities of subjects and the particularities of peoples are not due to a persistent will to become what they are. Identity is the result not of an action but of a history, in other words, of a process developed under conditions that behave haphazardly in the face of one's own pretensions.

The historical question "How did something become what it is at the moment?," posed to countries, cities, or people, is typically answered with an expression such as "that can only be explained historically." What does it means that something is only explicable through history (Lübbe 1973)? We are what we are because there was some accident, because something has prevented the completion of what was predictable, or because our intention was thwarted. This is the narrative side of history, where anomalous properties and singular combinations appear. We tell stories because we are not what we wanted to be or what we should wish we were.

From these considerations, we can understand the justification for continuously revising our past and rewriting history without accepting that it is treated as an object or given over to the illusion of the definitive. The historic investigation goes hand in hand with the changes of identity of the subjects that carry it out, in such a way that our own identity and other people's is once again defined according to these modifications. We rewrite our history and that of other people because the presentation of identity—ours and theirs—is a function of our history, through which we obtain our identity. The histories we tell have to be open to change because they change the open stories that we are.

From this perspective, we can also understand the conditions that make our affective identification with an "us" bearable and legitimate. Patriotism is by its very nature unstable. Patriotism is stretched across time, which is why it tends to include a reconsideration of its own history. But this duration is labile. The problem of patriotism is always its *detautologization* (Fuchs 1991), its transformation in specific circumstances. A patriot is in the same place to the extent that he or she moves, thus adapting to the temporalization of a society that is becoming more complex. In this way, the artificiality of the construction of any us with which we can identify becomes obvious.

We need a good deal of liberal consciousness to know how to become part of a community that is ours, with which we can identify or defend its right to freely control its destiny and, at the same time, be conscious of the artificiality of its construction, its nonnecessity, its involvement with other people's destiny.

Locals and Immigrants

One need not be especially critical or skeptical to know that the perception we have of things is not always correct. In the case of immigration, a phenomenon that configures the identity of locals and newcomers, there are two confusions that need to be cleared up before we can respond adequately to the question about who we are: we tend to believe that immigration presents a serious economic problem for host societies and that the influence goes in only one direction, that "they" only influence "us," both of which are at the heart of some concerns. What if in this matter it were also true that things are not what they seem?

Judging by particular discourses, some of them very electorally successful, we are subjected to a massive wave of immigration. On this matter, as with so many others, there are few numbers and a lot of specters. One of them refers to the cost of immigration, in other words, the increase in social expenses and the unemployment it provokes. It is important to confront this prejudice rather than resting all arguments on humanitarian reasons. Economic arguments do not have the prestige of moral reasons, but we should not scorn them when it comes to establishing what our duties for justice are. It could be that xenophobia, in addition to being ethically unjustifiable, is also economically ruinous.

Can we affirm that immigrants are responsible for the increase in unemployment? Polls reveal that the majority of people think so. Economists, on the other hand, are in relative agreement—something that is, by the way, unusual—that this is not the case (Chojnicki and Rago 2012). Immigration has very little impact on the unemployment rate of locals. It gives the impression that the weight of immigration on public debate is inversely proportional to its economic impact, which is relatively neutral.

Immigration tends to be thought of as increasing the market demand for jobs. If that is the case, immigration should be pushing salaries down as the amount of competition between "replaceable" workers increases. But this type of reasoning is very simple and does not take into account the complexity of the phenomenon. In the first place, immigration acts on supply, but also on demand. Immigrants help increase the final demand for goods and services, which stimulates economic activity and, consequently, employment. Immigrants are in a complementary, not a replacement, relationship with local-born workers (the rivalry is actually between old and new immigrants).

A similar prejudice refers to the supposed burden that immigrants represent for public finances. Our system of social protection is ascendant, in other words, it implies a transfer from younger to older people, particularly pensioners. The two areas of social protection that essentially assist older people—health care and pensions—now represent around 80 percent of social costs, while immigrants are grouped in the ages of greatest activity. The fact that immigrants increase certain social expenses is more than compensated by the reality that they are generally in an age group that pays more than they receive from the redistribution system. We must remember that immigrants also contribute to the financing of social protection through their contributions. In a pure accounting sense, we could evaluate their net contribution (the difference between contributions and benefits), which would allow us to question the eventual benefits of a reduction in immigration, as is sometimes defended. Of course, less immigration means lower social costs, but it also and especially means fewer contributions. In any case, a tightening of immigration policies will not help resolve our problem of budgetary deficits.

Epilogue ❦ 171

On the other hand, if immigrants run greater risks of increasing the expenses derived from unemployment or other government-provided services, they spend much less than locals on everything related to health and old age. In any case, if we took the logic of excluding those who represent the largest expenses for the social protection system to the extreme, we would also have to censure those who are unemployed, handicapped, or ill, which would place in question the very notion of social justice.

There are other clichés found in the emotions provoked by immigration and in many of the dominant discourses that prevent us from seeing part of reality. For example, the image of immigrants as a powerful threat in the face of our supposedly fragile identity. We are always told, either with fear or in celebration of new diversity, about the influence that immigrants have on the identity and the culture that takes them in, but we barely examine the influence that goes in the opposite direction. The question that is always raised is whether immigration, paired with low birth rates, will make European societies lose their identity when their cities, some people insist, seem increasingly like cities in Africa or Asia. The ideological xenophobia that fears "ethnic replacement" and the loss of the European identity and the liberal attitude that, with the best of intentions, defends the "integration" of new arrivals both see immigration as a phenomenon that acts upon the host country, but they barely reflect on the influence that immigration has on the countries and cultures of origin. What if we influence them as much as they influence us? Why not think about the fact that immigration, far from weakening our identity, is a way of spreading our values throughout the world?

In the first place, it is curious that such fears prevent us from seeing the radical asymmetry that characterizes the phenomenon of immigration. It would seem as if the roles of the strong and the weak were switched, with the threat coming from the undoubtedly weaker element in the relationship. First of all, immigrants are, in general, a minority in host societies and are more exposed to the culture of the locals than the locals are exposed to the culture brought by the immigrants. Secondly, immigrants, from the economic, social, and political point of view, are more of a dominated than a dominating group, and their influence on the culture of the host society is much less pronounced than the influence that goes in the other direction. Both of these factors make it clear that there are sufficient reasons to believe that those most affected by the encounter are the ones who immigrate, not those who receive them.

Immigrants are continuously exposed to the ideas, values, and practices of the society in which they live, in such a way that they can make them their own and transmit them to their communities of origin. The question is not so much whether the host society is changed, but knowing the extent to which, through emigrants, birth societies are exposed to the values on which the identity of the host society is founded. We should, therefore, consider immigration a two-way process, which offers emigrants' birth society a certain number of ideas or behaviors that they picked up in the host society. If we look at things in this way, immigrants would not only be introducing non-Western values and practices into Western countries; they would also be channeling things in the opposite direction, spreading Western values and practices to other parts of the world. Immigrants do not only send money home; they also share ideas and models of behavior. Given that immigrants are frequently considered success stories in their countries of origin, this allows societies to open themselves to the values and practices that led to that success. In this way, immigration can be an instrument of influence and cultural diffusion, but not in the direction we habitually believe.

We are prevented from understanding all the complexity and nuances of immigration because we still maintain a static conception of cultures and societies. "Integration" and "replacement" are the two terms that try to explain the relationship between cultures that collide with each other in a single direction. Conservatives and liberals tend to think that cultural differences are perpetuated through generations and would allow affected populations to reproduce independently from one another. They do not keep in mind the bidirectionality of their influences and the phenomena of mixing, the exogamy that tends to increase with the passing of time. Classifying people as local or foreign ends up cutting an arbitrary line through a continuum where there are not two populations but one, made up of people who present a large number of possible combinations in terms of origins. Given the dynamism and porousness of current societies, belonging to a single group is going to increasingly be the exception rather than the rule.

Examining the phenomenon of immigration in all its complexity is the best way of disposing of particular topics. Behind existing preconceptions, we tend to find a reality that has not been fully understood.

The Limits of Community

The huge increase in complexity sets in motion the desire to reduce it to a size that can be understood and governed. It is always worth demanding a restoration of what is lost and designing a melancholy protest in the face of the growing estrangement of social realities; it is also possible to construct communitarian enclaves of good sense connected by reciprocal confirmations, without any problematization.

The archetypal contrast made by Tönnies (1960 [1887]) between community and society—which has its own dualisms: organism versus artifact, comprehension versus contract—presents a typical antinomy of politics in the modern age, at least since the complaints in the Romantic period. Continuing this approach, the Husserlian concept of "lifeworld" has been, since 1926, the counterpoint that opposes social turbulence. The suggestion it exerts is probably due to the fact that its mere mention illuminates an area of familiarity and trustworthiness, a protective core. It symbolizes the opposite of everything that is complex and strange in the social structure, promising a balanced world in the midst of the confusion of the social system. In the face of the contractual artifice, the community is the place where we find images of the emphatic us, the connections and original identifications.

But it is not possible to close Pandora's box and imagine a simpler configuration of the world. Modern societies do not owe their strength to identifying determinants, but to resistance in the face of the hypostasis of a lost familiarity as well as the definitive determination of the social arena. If a society wants to remain free, it must reject all totalizing unity between the representative and those represented.

Taking the American Declaration of Independence as an example, Derrida showed the circular and contradictory nature of constitutional documents, in which "the people" sign that they are constituting themselves as a unitary subject through their signature. However, the people do not exist prior to their foundational act, an act that precedes the people as an authorizing agent. This strange event means that by signing, the people come into the world as a free and independent subject, as a possible signatory. Signing authorizes the signature (Derrida 1980, 66). In the us brought together in the foundational act, we mask an originating heterogeneity. "The people" is a declaring subject at the same time as it is an empirical group of still disparate individuals; the people establish a law to which they themselves do not submit. The unrepeatable and fictitious foundation represents nothing but the initial nonidentity that is broken into a continuous iteration. This impossible identity recalls that the foundation is not closed once and for all, that the communal is not original or present, previous or deducible, but something continuously displaced, extended, deferred. The heterogeneity of the community that founds itself forces it to always repeat its foundation again. "The collective subject is always in a state of continuing self-constitution, and the judgments it makes will have a reflective effect upon its own identity as a community" (Beiner 1983, 143).

In the heart of all constitutional order, of any democratic coexistence, there is an inconsistent us, a ripping and a contradiction, that continuously redefines in a provisional manner the standing of inclusion and exclusion. That is why politics cannot be monopolized by institutional realities, by the organization of society, and by ritualized statehood. Politics is instead a place in which a society acts upon itself and renews the appearance of its common public space. Society has not emerged from the collapse of a community; there is no originating division or first unification or innocence lost in collective life or an initial institution. This does not mean that the us does not exist at all, but that it is an unstable size, an open and mutable reality, taken by human beings at the design of destiny and situated in the area of what we do with our freedom.

EPISTEMOLOGY OF THE US

The Familiar and Unfamiliar

The us also has an epistemological dimension: we are the ones who know something in the face of those who do not know, those who understand something that others do not understand, to whom certain things are familiar and others strange, or we have a specific ability that differentiates us. The epistemological providence of the us has been formed in many diverse ways, and its flip side is the unfamiliar, the inexpert, or the ridiculous.

Human communities have always resisted recognizing their contingency, as if that recognition exposed them to a mortal storm. All cultural systems rebel again their own contingency by producing instruments that confirm their identity. Hymns, celebrations, genealogies, and rights are all rituals that compensate for an absent necessity and provide some ways of thinking removed from all arbitrariness, by virtue of which some practices are granted support and normality. Another prominent measure for this interior strengthening is the distance from the others, whose otherness is frequently sheathed in an incompressible unfamiliarity. To make their form of life itself appear natural, they marginalize other forms of life, sometimes even pushing it toward monstrousness. This alienation is sometimes almost inoffensive, as is revealed in what we consider ridiculous, in the realm of the laughable. Perhaps that explains the abundance of jokes that come from the fragmentation of the world, such as intercultural misunderstandings or tribal scorn (there is no country or locality that has not created a geographic imaginary—generally, the immediate neighbor—that functions as the space where the ridiculous occurs).

Social systems are disentangled in a familiar realm that is always strange for others. However, the magnitude of what is familiar is mobile because there are processes of estrangement, of a loss of evidence, confidence, and familiarity. In ancient societies, the realm of the familiar had the same extension as any known society and the unfamiliar was anything that did not allow itself to be reduced to that arena. Now, under modern conditions, it turns out that the unfamiliar is ever more socially present. There is no longer any need to abandon society to go beyond the limits of the known; there are exclusive familiarities, like the space of privacy, and unknown magnitudes that we can access, through investigation or travel. The distinction between the familiar and the unfamiliar is as moveable as the observation; we also know that the familiar is not an ontological but a cultural scale, that it is familiar from a particular point of view and unfamiliar from another.

Our knowledge starts at a situation; we are part of a particular learning community, but reason knows that position as well and can in some ways transcend it. Creating a certain distance from our own reality makes it possible for us to observe our situation from the outside. It is the traditional thinking of Montesquieu's *Persian Letters*, continued by a long literary tradition in which the narrator adopts extraterritoriality, such as someone who is returning, a child, someone who is ill or a misfit. It is reasonable to institute forms of dealing with the world that take into account the plurality of perspectives thus establishing new opportunities for the exercise of the tolerance that Luhmann and Fuchs have summed up in the expression "cultivated incongruence" (1989, 223). The only human identity is one that allows the incongruous to appear, that takes into consideration what others say of you, that is concerned about exclusions they might be permitting, that is capable of imagining itself differently, that laughs at itself. Taking the unfamiliar into account means developing a special gaze for ruptures and paradoxes that, in spite of everything, exist within the self-evident. The cultural experience of the unfamiliar always means a confrontation with possible alternatives to one's own life and leads to putting our reality to the test. The unfamiliar is a reserve to enrich and correct the limitation of one's own positions.

In this sense, the epistemological usefulness of comical situations stems from the knowledge of our own relativity: the experience that something that is taken to be valid is not valid at all times or in all contexts. Funny things always imply some relativizing of prevailing criteria, a small subversion; the measure of what is correct is not absolutely stable, but culturally and historically variable. This can be seen in the example of the person who attends the burial of someone in a neighboring town and asks: is the tradition here to cry in the house of the deceased or do we wait until we get to the cemetery? So the instrument to exclude and make ridiculous, placed at the service of self-relativization, is also very useful when it comes to managing one's own contingency. Any grouping is always threatened by the possibility of looking ridiculous from a particular perspective.

Experts and Novices

The us of the experts is an epistemological us from which power and exclusion have always been configured. The elites remind us of it when it is time for big decisions, but daily experience does too ("only to be opened by an expert," "consult your pharmacist," and so on). Expert authority is invoked to legitimize, which tends to mean that it undermines or excludes those who are supposedly not experts.

As with so many other differences that I have been examining here, the distinction between the knowledgeable and the ignorant has never stopped existing, but in a democratic society this difference is constantly needed to sanction the legitimacy of the society, overwhelmed by others' desires to participate and be heard. The current public discussion of scientific subjects, for example, does not mean that scientific competence no longer makes sense, but that the distinction between those who are on the inside and those who are on the outside of the scientific disciplines has softened. We no longer live in an age when experts discuss indisputable data and use their knowledge to put an end to all controversy. In a knowledge society, people possess greater cognitive abilities. New organizations and interest groups emerge that help weaken the authority of experts. What was at some point an exoteric power of knowledge is now publicly debated, controlled, and regulated. The goal of a democracy of knowledge is to treat everyone as citizens who are equally responsible for political decisions, without erasing their different degrees of competence.

We thus have a substantial problem, which is the social reintegration of science when we know that there are too many important matters at play to leave them exclusively in the hands of specialists. In our collective experiments, the division of labor where the figure of the expert is the mediator between the production of knowledge and society does not work.

New information and communication technologies have transformed our lives into a type of "consecration of the amateur," a society of hobbyists, a democratization of competencies (Flichy 2010). Without needing authorization or instructions, the new image of the citizen is that of an *amateur* who informs him- or herself, openly expresses opinions, and develops new forms of commitment; that is why he or she distrusts experts as much as representatives.

Distributed intelligence challenges the experts, to the extent that, from the beginning, it prepares anyone to access knowledge.

In a knowledge society, there is an increase in intermediate-level knowledge, the free circulation of information, the ability to communicate one's own opinions. For this reason, the new circulation of knowledge and competencies has huge democratizing potential. Democracy arose precisely against the monopoly of power and as a universalization of the competency of governing; this new democratization is now based on the fact that technological abilities let anyone acquire the ability to watch, control, and judge at any time.

In a knowledge society, the states are no longer faced with an unformed mass of novices but with distributed intelligence, a more demanding citizenry, and a humanity of observers, which includes a large number of international organisms that not only evaluate them, but frequently have more and better expert knowledge than the states. To put it clearly, the person who is in charge is no longer the one who knows the most. In any case, and also for epistemological reasons, it is important for science not to discredit urges or irritations that come from the "outside" as ignorance or hysteria. It may be that the experts are not the ones who know the most either and that, when it comes to epistemological questions, it is better for there to be greater flexibility on the border that divides the experts from the masses.

THE PRACTICE OF THE US

Our Common Goods

If the truth is difficult to pass on to an us placed in the role of experts, something similar occurs with goodness, even if it is only because, in a world of shared destinies, of contagions, and of common vulnerabilities, it is increasingly difficult to understand the good as something that belongs to someone specific, in an exclusive fashion.

In the first place, a complex society, in which there is profound and irreversible pluralism, does not allow a substantialist definition of the common good. The subordination of all individual selfishness to a "group good" is something that is not produced in an intuitive or automatic fashion. It could be said that this ambiguity is constitutive of our societies and that politics consists precisely in articulating this space of discussion, since it is not guarded by any indisputable authority, protecting itself in that way from any attempt at monopolization. No one has an interpretative monopoly about the common good at their disposal, nor can they dependably represent everyone. In the last instance, it is a principle that limits more than it justifies, when it begins by preventing anyone from appropriating the general interest, universality. It exercises, in a manner of speaking, the function of having all of society in view without allowing anyone to take it over. Every concrete determination of the common good inevitably implies some type of inclusion and exclusion (the us does not in fact generally coincide with the everyone). It is important to recognize this fact precisely so we can appraise it.

We find ourselves in a historic moment in which this extension of self-interest seems especially necessary. The common good has lost its fixed reference to a stable framework of identification and management, which could be represented by the nation-state or a clearly delimited community; it overflows and distinguishes itself, at the same time as the subjects to which it may refer expand and fragment. There are movements that force us to consider that we are more than those who are here (emigration, processes of integration in broader political spaces, globalization), while we sometimes encounter the demand to single out and pay attention to pluralities that were not previously on our radar (processes of decentralization, attention to minorities, affirmative action). Global challenges have weakened the distinction between here and there, us and them, now and later tremendously. That is why it is as difficult as it is urgent to refashion and make operative the concept of the common good.

The identification of the beneficiary us is especially difficult in spaces that are fluid, transnational, that are neither isolated nor enclosed with indisputable limits for state or communitarian enclaves. There are always others who can argue about the negative effects of our common good (the requirement for external justification), and there continues to be more and more internal plurality in new social units, which makes it more difficult to achieve consensus (internal differentiation). What is common is not an indisputable size, but is always contextualized and elastic, just like the limits of those we consider one of us.

The question that Claus Offe (2001) formulated, with critical intention: for whom is the common good good? In other words, what community are we talking about, who belongs to the chosen ones, could the groups be divided differently nowadays, indicating the common goods of humanity that no longer favor some over others, in the same way that shared threats make no distinctions or provisos? The presence of these common goods makes it increasingly more unreasonable to think of the climate, financial stability, and security as goods that belong to only some people or to pursue these goods at the expense of someone else. In the age of growing interdependence, there continue to be exclusive interests, of course, but the interweaving of collective destinies prevents us from defining our good as the opposite of other people's bad or thinking that we can achieve our own good without promoting, even laterally and involuntarily, the goods of others.

Who Is Our Neighbor?

The term "complicity" has become part of the common language. It always used to indicate conspiracy, collaboration, intrigue, or cover-ups of a crime. Now it is a more innocent word that refers to a kind camaraderie. This slippage may, however, denounce the connection that exists between solidarity and conspiracy, that the us is infrequently constituted against others, friends are friends because they have common enemies, and there is no coalition without exclusion.

Something similar may happen with the current exaltation of proximity, which has the undeniable prestige of its moral and religious resonance—responsibilities toward others or the value of closeness. But in an age of interdependence, the banishing of distances, and communicative instantaneousness, proximity leaves open the question of whether it is not too little, a type of complicity with those who are similar at the expense of those who are different and distant, but with whom, nevertheless, we have increased interactions and, therefore, increased responsibilities.

The race to proximity is revealed by the fact that there is an increase in appeals to value the close against the far, the concrete and different in the face of the universal or abstract. Close relationships correct the verticality of social relationships and impersonal social rules, which are viewed as too general. To understand the extent to which this emphasis is a novelty, we must keep in mind that until recently proximity bred distrust. Proximity has always evoked privileges and inequalities, arbitrariness, and favoritism. The founding myths of modernization have functioned in exactly the opposite direction than what we observe today: modernity came from the center; distance was synonymous with impartiality, efficiency, and legitimacy. In this context, it is very significant for current transformations that certain public policies that historically constituted the "local" (the police, justice, or education) now emphasize proximity.

But proximity is full of artifice. We should remember that proximity is not simply something given, but a social construction and is often reduced to an impression of proximity produced by actors who successfully carry out their rapprochement strategies. That is why it is not unusual for there to be experts and businesses specialized in producing those strategies. The uses and rituals of proximity make us sometimes confuse proximity with notoriety and visibility, with the suggestion of proximity constructed by means of communication. There is a proximity "effect" that is pure staging, media construction, false closeness, especially after the moment in which it can be produced without the effective corporal presence through the means of communication.

On the other hand, proximity is not a physical reality or an unquestioned dimension, especially with our virtualized and media spaces, without territorial determinism, in a globalized world with growing mobility. Many social battles are carried out around the attempt for proximity and its definition. Proximity has become the central ideology by which multiple actors work on their own legitimation. But what is, strictly speaking, closest? How does one define closeness and distance? Those who work in favor of proximity should not forget that, in the new configuration of social spaces, proximity does not mean the suppression of distance. There are close things that are far and proximities that are very distant.

Those of Us Who Live in the Present

If, from the spatial point of view, the category of proximity is questionable, something similar is taking place from a temporal perspective. Could it not be that this preference for proximity is part of a fixation on the present that establishes a coalition of the living in the face of the rights of future generations? Are we not then facing a temporal version of the privilege that some people want to realize in space, a type of temporal colonialism? In both cases, there is a complicity of the us at the expense of a third party: if, in the exclusivism of spaces, it was *the one from outside*, in temporal imperialism it is *the one who comes later* who bears the expenses of our preference. The externalization of the impacts of the present onto a future that does not concern us is converted into true irresponsibility. We enjoy a type of impunity in the temporal zone of the future where we can recklessly deplete other people's time or expropriate other people's future. Those of us who live in the present are "squatters" on their future. We are performing what Alexander Kluge has called "the assault of the present on the rest of time." The more we live for our present, the less capable we will be of understanding and respecting the "nows" of other people.

When the consequences of actions are extended through space until they affect people on the other side of the world and through time until they condition the future of people near and far, a good many ideas and practices require profound revision. Both spatial and temporal interconnectedness should be taken into thoughtful consideration: anything that implicitly conditions the future should be made transparent and the object of democratic processes. A broadening of our temporal horizon is one of our most basic moral and political imperatives. In summary, this means we can no longer think of the future as the garbage collector of the present, as an "unloading zone" (Koselleck), a place where unresolved problems are sent so as to free the present of them.

But the realization that the destiny of various generations is as intermingled as the spaces of globalization calls into question our occupation of the future. If the responsibility for the future has turned into an acute problem, it is because there has been an increase in the number of future scenarios we must keep in mind during present-day decision-making and planning sessions. There is no legitimate us if we do not weigh issues of justice when examining the things that are conveyed from one generation to the next. These transfers include legacies and memories, but also expectations and possibilities that are handed over to future generations, in terms of physical, environmental, human, technological, and institutional capital.

Generational interdependence demands a new type of social contract. In accordance with the new realities of spatial and temporal interconnectedness, it no longer makes sense to understand the social contract in an exclusivist or contemporaneous sense. In other words, it cannot be limited to the us of one specific community or to those who are currently alive. The model of social contract that only regulates obligations between contemporaries must be expanded to include future subjects with whom we find ourselves in complete asymmetry. Questions of intergenerational justice are not resolved with a logic of reciprocity, but with an ethics of transmission.

The first reflection imposed on us by this new conception of the world is a decision about whom we should consider our "neighbor." In other words, we make the shift from a responsibility toward "close relations" (Paul Ricoeur) to the responsibility for "more distant things" (Nietzsche). We must understand that a neighbor does not mean only those who are closest in space or in time. Our horizon of reference must be expanded in such a way that intergenerational justice is not limited to simple transfers between contiguous generations. The principle of responsibility is oriented specifically toward the distant future and to an us that cannot be legitimately constituted as close at the expense of those who are "distant," which requires their inclusion in some way.

THE CONVERGENCE OF THE US

The Reiteration of the Question About Us

Every examination about the responsibilities that connect us links back to the question about who we are. Human beings have responded to this question in various ways throughout history, and our answers have become inflexible because of changes in social conditions, technological possibilities, and the consciousness we have of ourselves. The great advances of humanity have come from the iteration of that question and from acting accordingly once we discovered that we are more than we thought, that there are exclusions in every social order. Who can be one of us or stop counting as one of us?

Then we realize that there are more or less of us and we belong to different degrees, depending on particular conditions that are modified over time. Human liberty always implies an ability to remove ourselves from the places where we are part of one group and call for another type of grouping. We also discover that there are "others," women, foreigners, subordinates, that do not enjoy the same rights. Any organized discourse distributes the opportunities to assert oneself unevenly. This problem is not solved by simply making sure there is a balanced organization of power between speakers. There are also voices that are systematically or indirectly excluded, differences that cannot make themselves heard or that do not match the dominant criteria.

In the space of globalization, with porous and multiple identities, with complex interactions, where contamination and interdependence rule, when everything is transferred and there is no protective core, the "us" is characterized by great indetermination. In a space of communal good and evil, any delimitation that is too rigid between us and them is inappropriate. We should think of ourselves in a potentially universal manner. At the same time, we must construct new systems of responsibility that are operative and reflect complexity in an interdependent world.

The nation-state has been a formidable response to this question about who we are. We have become nationals of our country, with interests that clearly contrast with the interests of foreigners, others affected by the same problems, inhabitants of the same space bound by fixed borders, represented according to criteria of democratic legitimacy, with identical rights and responsibilities, in a particular realm of decision-making and solidarity. This framework has clearly been inadequate for some time now. The nation-state, while it forms policy for the us, is overwhelmed by global poverty, the obligation to protect others, the pressing need for common goods, the complexity of global agreements on climatic or financial matters. Globalization has produced an authentic national justice that is out of balance. It is not necessarily the same as the neoliberal jungle, but represents the demand to present rights and responsibilities in a new context.

The principal theories of justice have had as their starting point the principle that obligations of justice are only valid for those who live within a particular political community or under the same constitution. In reality, we should think that the demands of justice are previous to the institutions that channel them (Young 2010, 329). That is why we should reiterate the question of the us in an innovative fashion, which currently, when the us is no longer sufficiently contained by the nation-state, means thinking about justice globally, discovering humanity beyond the nation-state, moving from sovereignty to responsibility.

The largest part of our reciprocal obligations are neither explained nor managed within state frameworks. Justice and injustice are ever more conditioned by global structures and require actions on that level. Poverty, for example, is explained not only by local causes but by factors of a global order. Something analogous occurred with the responsibility of military protection and intervention, which are increased in a more interdependent world. The revision of the us that is secured by state sovereignty implies overcoming mere juxtaposition or indifferent coexistence. The universalization of human rights, the slow ascent of the principle of universal jurisdiction, and the reinforcement of international integration are indicators that point in the direction of a transnational humanism, of humanity as the us that is constituted as a reference point in an interdependent world. From this point of view, we are, increasingly, transnationals.

The Construction of Universality

We are almost never everyone. In the first place, because there is an inevitable and generally innocent particularness: those aspects of our identity that we cannot choose or modify. We cannot all be born in one place or fully change (in spite of the growing technological possibilities) our corporal condition. The second plane of the relationship between us and them refers to conditions of access, inclusion, and expulsion from a community, where contingency is greater and, therefore, so is modifiability. The third has to do with the tension that points toward humanity as a whole. At this level, to a certain extent and in agreement with what is in play, we can and should be everyone. This possibility, responsibility, or aspiration is referenced by objectives of global governance, transnational obligations, and even certain responsibilities that go further than the internal solidarity of our species and make us something more than us as humans. All the debates between patriotism and cosmopolitism turn on the articulation of these three planes, and many misunderstandings stem from not differentiating them sufficiently.

Universality, humanism, and cosmopolitism should be thought of as constructions and not as acquisitions, as horizons that are pursued, and not as identifications that are monopolized. The problem is often not that we do not want to be universal, but that we believe we can become universal immediately, saving ourselves the effort of constructing it. We humans tend to identify our particularity with the universal too easily. There is no worse particularity than the one that does not recognize itself as such. Therefore, for example, during the First World War, Max Weber demanded support for the German Empire in the name of *Kultur*, while Émile Durkheim asked for the same for France in the name of *Civilisation*. In both cases, there was an attempt at totality, a totalizing us that believed it represented universality perfectly. However, there is no construction of universality where there is no recognition of the particularity of each of us, the unique headquarters where the tension toward universality can be activated.

The current world offers new possibilities toward the construction of the communal precisely because a dense interdependence rules it. We share the same risks, sovereign action is ineffective, unilateral protections are insufficient, immunity is revealed to be illusory, the distinction between what is ours and what is other people's is as problematic as the distinction between us and them or the distinction we establish between internal and external. I have used the label "world without outlying areas" for this expansion of references that weaken at the same time the proximity of what is genuinely ours. In a world like this, there are more things that are ours, more realities that concern us, than we are accustomed to thinking. The lack of consideration toward what does not seem to be ours is an absurdity that endangers us, which is why cooperation imposes itself as the most intelligent strategy. In the same way as globalization converts our identity into something more porous and open, our destinies are also increasingly intertwined.

Inclusion becomes an essential key to the treatment of global problems. A true global politics should begin by unmasking illegitimate representations of the us of humanity, the institutional appropriations that are not sufficiently inclusive. How many global institutions represent some people better than others or have hardened into democratically unjustifiable asymmetries? A "politics of humanity" could be defined in this respect as the project of restoring the balance between those who decide and those who suffer. The legitimacy of any us—of any demarcation or differentiation of interests—depends on placing ourselves on that line of tension. It is not necessary for us to be all (which is not possible or good), but we should always question whether we are everyone who is here and whether everyone who is here is us.

REFERENCES

Aeschylus. 1985. *Prometeo encadenado*. Madrid: Gredos.
Agnew, John. 1994. "The Territorial Trap: The Geographical Assumptions of International Relations Theory." *Review on International Political Economy* 1 (1): 53–80.
Albrow, Martin. 1996. *The Global Age: State and Society Beyond Modernity*. Cambridge: Polity.
Aldy, Joseph, and Robert Stavins. 2009. *Post-Kyoto International Climate Policy*. Cambridge: Cambridge University Press.
Anders, Günther. 1956. *Die Antiquiertheit des Menschen*. München: Beck.
Anderson, Malcolm. 1997. *Frontiers: Territory and State Formation in the Modern World*. Cambridge: Polity.
Andreas, Peter. 2000. *Border Games: Policing the US-Mexico Divide*. Ithaca: Cornell University Press.
Badie, Bertrand. 2002. *La diplomatie des droits de l'homme*. Paris: Fayard.
———. 2004. *L'impuissance de la puissance: Essai sur les nouvelles relations internationales*. Paris: Fayard.
Balibar, Étienne. 1998. "The Borders of Europe." In *Cosmopolitics: Thinking and Feeling Beyond the Nation*, edited by Pheng Cheah and Bruce Robbins, 216–233. Minneapolis: University of Minnesota Press.
Barbrook, Richard, and Andy Cameron. 2001. "Californian Ideology." In *Crypto Anarchy, Cyberstates, and Pirate Utopias*, edited by Peter Ludlow, 362–387. Cambridge, Mass.: MIT Press.

Bauman, Zygmunt. 2002a. *Society Under Siege*. Cambridge: Polity.
———. 2002b. "Reconnaissance Wars of the Planetary Frontierland." *Theory, Culture and Society* 19 (4): 39–55.
———. 2006. *Liquid Fear*. Cambridge: Polity.
———. 2007. *Liquid Times: Living in an Age of Uncertainty*. Cambridge: Polity.
Beauvallet, Maya. 2009. *Les stratégies absurdes: Comment faire pire en croyant faire mieux*. Paris: Seuil.
Beck, Ulrich. 1997. *Was ist Globalisierung? Irrtümer des Globalismus—Antworten auf Globalisierung*. Frankfurt: Suhrkamp.
———. 2002. *Macht und Gegenmacht im globalen Zeitalter: Neue weltpolitische Ökonomie*. Frankfurt: Suhrkamp.
———. 2006. "Living in the World Risk Society." *Economy and Society* 35 (3): 329–345.
———. 2007. *Weltrisikogesellschaft*. Frankfurt: Suhrkamp.
———. 2008. *Die Neuvermessung der Ungleichheit unter den Menschen*. Frankfurt: Suhrkamp.
Beck, Ulrich, and Edgar Grande. 2004. *Das kosmopolitische Europa: Gesellschaft und Politik in der Zweiten Moderne*. Frankfurt: Suhrkamp.
Beiner, Ronald. 1983. *Political Judgement*. Chicago: University of Chicago Press.
Beitz, Charles. 1979. *Political Theory and International Relations*. Princeton: Princeton University Press.
Bhagwati, Jagdish N. 1986. "U.S. Inmigration Policy: What Next?" In *Essays on Legal and Illegal Immigration*, edited by Susan Pozo. Kalamazoo: Upjohn Institute for Employment Research.
Bigo, Didier. 2006. "Protection: Security, Territory and Population." In *The Politics of Protection: Sites of Insecurity and Political Agency*, edited by Jef Huysmans, Andrew Dobson, and Raia Prokhovnik, 84–100. New York: Routledge.
Boltanski, Luc, and Ève Chiapello. 1999. *Le Nouvel Esprit du capitalisme*. Paris: Gallimard.
Bourke, Joanna. 2005. *Fear: A Cultural History*. Emeryville, Calif.: Shoemaker and Hoard.
Brossat, Alain. 2003. *La démocratie immunitaire*. Paris: La Dispute.
Brown, Wendy. 2010. *Walled States, Waning Sovereignty*. New York: Zone.

Buchanan, Allen. 2000. "Rawls's Law of Peoples: Rules for a Vanished Westphalian World." *Ethics* 110 (4): 697–721.

Cardon, Dominique. 2010. *La démocratie internet: Promeses et limites*. Paris: Seuil.

Castells, Manuel. 2003. *La era de la información*, vol. 2. Madrid: Alianza.

———. 2011. *Communication Power*. Oxford: Oxford University Press.

Cerny, Philip G. 1994. "The Dynamics of Financial Globalization: Technology, the Market Structure and Policy Response." *Policy Sciences* 27 (4): 319–342.

Cerruti, Furio. 2007. *Global Challenges for Leviathan: A Political Philosophy of Nuclear Weapons and Global Warming*. Lanham, Md.: Lexington Books.

Charolles, Valérie. 2008. *Croissance, inflation, chômage, crise financière . . . Et si les chiffres disaent pas toute la vérité: Chroniques économico-philosophiques*. Paris: Fayard.

Chojnicki, Xavier, and Lionel Rago. 2012. *On entend dire que . . . l'immigration coute cher à la France: Qu'en pensent les économistes?* Paris: Eyrolles/Les Echos.

Chomsky, Noam. 2002. *Pirates and Emperors, Old and New Terrorism in the Real World*. London: Pluto.

Cicero, Marcus Tullius. 1887. *De officiis*. Translated by Andrew P. Peabody. Boston: Little, Brown.

Czada, Roland. 2000. "Legitimation durch Risiko: Gefahrenvorsorge und Katastrophenschutz als Staatsaufgaben." *Politische Vierteljahresschrift* 31:319–345.

Dahl, Robert. 1994. "A Democratic Dilemma: System Effectiveness Versus Citizen Participation." *Political Science Quarterly* 109 (1): 23–34.

Davis, Angela. 2005. *Abolition Democracy: Beyond Empire, Prisons, and Torture*. New York: Seven Stories Press.

Deleuze, Gilles, and Félix Guattari. 1972. "Traité de nomadologie." In *Mille Plateaux: Capitalisme et schizophrénie*, 434–527. Paris: Editions de Minuit.

Delmas-Marty, Mireille. 2010. *Libertés et sureté dans un monde dangereux*. Paris: Seuil.

Delumeau, Jean. 1989. *El miedo en Occidente*. Madrid: Taurus.

Deng, Francis Mading, Donald Rothchild, and William Zartman. 1996. *Sovereignty as Responsibility*. Washington, D.C.: Brookings Institution Press.

Derrida, Jacques. 1980. "Nietzsches Otobiographie oder Politik des Eigennamens." *Fugen: Deutsch-Französisches Jahrbuch für Text-Analytik*: 64–98.

———. 1993. *Spectres de Marx*. Paris: Gallimard.

———. 2001. *Foi et savoir*. Paris: Seuil.

Dewey, John. (1927) 1988. "The Public and Its Problems." In *The Later Works of John Dewey*, vol. 2, edited by Jo Ann Boydston, 235–372. Carbondale: Southern Illinois University Press.

Easterbrook, Don. 2007. "Réchauffement de la planète: Qui perd, qui gagne?" *Problèmes économiques*: 24–31.

Elias, Norbert. 1996. *Was ist Soziologie?* Weinheim: Juventa.

Esposito, Roberto. 2002. *Immunitas*. Torino: Einaudi.

Flichy, Patrice. 2010. *Sacre de l'amateur*. Paris: Seuil.

Foucault, Michel. 1975. *Survellir et punir*. Paris: Gallimard.

Fraser, Nancy. 1990. *Rethinking the Public Sphere: A Contribution to the Critique of Actually Existing Democracy*. Durham: Duke University Press.

Fuchs, Peter. 1991. "Vaterland, Patriotismus und Moral: Zur Semantik gesellschaftlicher Einheit." *Zeitschrift für Soziologie* 2:89–103.

Fung, Archon, Mary Graham, and David Weil. 2007. *Full Disclosure, the Perils and Promise of Transparency*. Cambridge: Cambridge University Press.

Garcés, Marina. 2011. "La pregunta por un mundo común." In *Las palabras del verbo (filosófico)*, edited by Manuel Cruz, 105–125. Barcelona: Herder.

Geithner, Timothy. 2008. "Robust and Stable System Is Goal of US." Interview, *Financial Times*, March 31, 2008.

Giddens, Anthony. 2002. *A Runaway World: How Globalisation Is Reshaping Our Lives*. London: Profile Books.

———. 2009. *The Politics of Climate Change*. Cambridge: Polity.

Gosse, Philip. (1932) 1989. *History of Piracy*. New Mexico: Rio Grande Classic.

Grande, Edgar, and Thomas Risse. 2000. "Bridging the Gap: Konzeptionelle Anforderungen an die politikwissenschaftliche Analyse von Globalisierungsprozessen." *Zeitschrift für Internationale Beziehung* 7:235–266.

Grotius, Hugo. (1606) 2006. *Commentary on the Law of Prize and Booty*. Edited by Martine Julia van Ittersum. Indianapolis: Liberty Fund.

Habermas, Jürgen. 1996. *Die postnationale Konstellation: Politische Essays*. Frankfurt: Suhrkamp.

———. 2011. *Zur Verfassung Europas—ein Essay*. Berlin: Suhrkamp.

Hardin, Garret. 1968. "The Tragedy of Commons." *Science* 162 (3859): 1243–1248.

Hardt, Michael, and Antonio Negri. 2000. *Multitude: War and Democracy in the Age of Empire*. Cambridge, Mass.: Harvard University Press.

Held, David. 2000. *A Globalizing World? Culture, Economics, Politics*. London: Routledge.

———. 2005. "Democratic Accountability and Political Effectiveness from a Cosmopolitan Perspective." In *Global Governance and Public Accountability*, edited by David Held and Mathias Koenig-Archibugi, 240–267. Oxford: Blackwell.

Held, David, and Anthony McGrew, eds. 2002. *Governing Globalisation: Power, Authority, and Global Governance*. Cambridge: Polity.

Heller-Roazen, Daniel. 2009. *The Enemy of All: Piracy and the Law of Nations*. New York: Zone.

Hill, Christopher. 1973. *The World Turned Upside Down: Radical Ideas During the English Revolution*. London: Temple Smith.

Hindman, Matthew. 2009. *The Myth of Digital Democracy*. Princeton: Princeton University Press.

Hirst, Paul. 2005. *Space and Power*. Cambridge: Polity.

Hobbes, Thomas. (1651) 2010. *Leviathan*. Edited by Ian Shapiro. New Haven: Yale University Press.

Höffe, Otfried. 1999. *Demokratie im Zeitalter der Globalisierung*. München: Beck.

Homer-Dixon, Thomas. 2006. *Catastrophe, Creativity, and the Renewal of Civilisation*. Washington: Island Press.

Innerarity, Daniel. 2004. *La sociedad invisible*. Madrid: Espasa.

Jackson, Robert. 1990. *Quasi-States: Sovereignty, International Relations and the Third World*. Cambridge: Cambridge University Press.

Johns, Adrian. 2009. *Piracy: The Intellectual Property Wars from Gutenberg to Gates*. Chicago: University of Chicago Press.

Jonas, Hans. 1979. *Das Prizip Verantwortung: Versuch einer Ethik für die technologischen Zivilisation*. Frankfurt: Insel.

———. 1984. *Das Prinzip Verantwortung—Versuch einer Ethik für die technologische Zivilisation*. Suhrkamp, Frankfurt.

Jones, Reece. 2012. *Border Walls: Security and the War on Terror in the United States, Israel and India*. London: Zed.

Joshi, Vijay, and Urjit Patel. 2009. "India and Climate Change Mitigation." In *The Economics and Politics of Climate Change*, edited by Dieter Helm and Cameron Hepburn, 167–196. Oxford: Oxford University Press, 2009.

Julius, A. J. 2006. "Nagel's Atlas." *Philosophy and Public Affairs* 34 (2): 176–192.

Kant, Immanuel. 1968a. *Zum ewigen Frieden, Werke: Akademie Textausgabe*, vol. 6. Berlin: De Gruyter.

———. 1968b. *Kritik der reinen Vernunft, Werke*. Edited by Preussische Akademie der Wissenschaften. Berlin: Walter de Gruyter. The translation of this text is from *Critique of Pure Reason*, translated by J. M. D. Meiklejohn and published by Collier in New York in 1901.

Kaul, Inge, Pedro Conceiçao, Katell Le Goulven, and Ronald U. Mendoza. 2003. *Providing Global Public Goods: Managing Globalization*. Oxford: Oxford University Press.

Keen, Andrew. 2008. *Le Culte de l'amateur: Comment l'internet tue notre culture*. Paris: Scali.

Keohane, Robert O. 1984. *After Hegemony: Cooperation and Discord in the World Political Economy*. Princeton: Princeton University Press.

Keohane, Robert O., and Joseph S. Nye Jr. 1998. "Power and Interdependence in the Information Age." *Foreign Affairs* 77 (5): 81–94.

Klein, Naomi. 2000. *No Logo*. London: Flamingo.

Lane, Robert E. 1966. "The Decline of Politics and Ideology in a Knowledgeable Society." *American Sociological Review* 31 (5): 649–662.

Latour, Bruno. 1999. *Politiques de la nature*. Paris: La Découverte.

Leadbeater, Charles, and Paul Miller. 2000. *The Pro-Am Revolution: How Enthusiasts Are Changing Our Economy and Society*. London: Demos.

Lemarchand, Frédérick. 2003. "Vers des sociétés épidémiques?" In *Dictionnaire des Risques*, edited by Y. Dupont. Paris: Armand Colin.

Lessig, L. 1999. *Code and Other Laws of Cyberspace*. New York: Basic Books.

Lesson, Peter T. 2009. *The Hidden Economy of Pirates*. Princeton: Princeton University Press.

Lübbe, Hermann. 1973. "Was heißt 'Das kann man nur historisch erkären?'" *X. Deutscher Kongreß für Philosophie*, edited by K. Hübner and A. Menne, 207–216. Hamburg: Meiner.

Luhmann, Niklas. 1981. "Wie ist soziale Ordnung möglich?" In *Gesellschaftstruktur und Semantik*, 2:195–285. Frankfurt: Suhrkamp.

Luhmann, Niklas, and Peter Fuchs. 1989. *Reden und Schweigen*. Frankfurt: Suhrkamp.

Macpherson, Crawford Brough. 1964. *The Political Theory of Possessive Individualism*. Oxford: Oxford University Press.

Maquiavelo [Machiavelli], Nicolás. 1987. *Discursos sobre la primera década de Tito Livio*. Madrid: Alianza.

Margalit, Avishai. 2009. "Any Ideology That Fails to Engage with Our Psychology Is Doomed to Failure." Interview, *Metropolis*, Summer.

Martins, Rui Cunha. 2007. *El método de la frontera: Radiografía histórica de un dispositivo contemporáneo*. Salamanca: Ediciones Universidad de Salamanca.

Mayntz, Renate. 2009. *Über Governance: Institutionen und Prozesse politischer Regelung*. Frankfurt: Campus.

Morozov, Evgeny. 2011. *The Net Delusion: The Dark Side of Internet Freedom*. New York: PublicAffairs.

Neyrat, Frédéric. 2004. *Surexposés*. Paris: Lignes et Manifestes.

Offe, Claus. 2001. "Wessen Wohl ist das Gemeinwohl?" In *Die Öffentlichkeit der Vernunft und die Vernunft der Öffentlichkeit: Festschrift für Jürgen Habermas*, edited by Lutz Wingert and Klaus Günther, 459–488. Frankfurt: Suhrkamp.

Olson, Mancur. 1971. *The Logic of Collective Action*. Cambridge, Mass.: Harvard University Press.

Palan, Ronen. 2003. *The Offshore World: Sovereign Markets, Virtual Places, and Nomad Millionaires*. Ithaca: Cornell University Press.

Paterson, Matthew. 1996. *Global Warming and Global Politics*. London: Routledge.

Pogge, Thomas W. 1989. *Realizing Rawls*. Ithaca: Cornell University Press.

———. 2001. *Global Justice*. Oxford: Blackwell.

Pulcini, Elena. 2009. *La cura del mundo: Paura and responsabilità nell'età globale*. Torino: Bollati Boringhieri.

Rawls, John. 1971. *A Theory of Justice*. Cambridge, Mass.: Harvard University Press.

———. 1999. *Law of Peoples*. Cambridge, Mass.: Harvard University Press.

Reinicke, Wolfgang H. 1998. *Global Public Policy: Governing Without Government?* Washington, D.C.: Brookings Institution Press.

Robertson, Roland. 1992. *Globalization: Social Theory and Global Culture.* London: Sage.

Robin, Corey. 2004. *Fear: The History of a Political Idea.* Oxford: Oxford University Press.

Rosanvallon, Pierre. 2008. *La légitimité démocratique: Impartialité, réflexivité, proximité.* Paris: Seuil.

Rosenau, James. 1990. *Turbulence in World Politics: A Theory of Change and Continuity.* Princeton: Princeton University Press.

———. 1999. "Toward an Ontology for Global Governance." In *Approaches to Global Governance Theory,* edited by Martin Hewson and Timothy J. Sinclair, 287–301. Albany: State University of New York Press, 1999.

Rosenau, James Nathan, and Ernst-Otto Czempiel, eds. 1992. *Governance Without Government: Order and Change in World Politics.* Cambridge: Cambridge University Press.

Röttgers, Kurt. 1983. *Texte und Menschen.* Würzburg: Königshauser und Neumann.

Roubini, Nouriel, and Stephan Mihn. 2011. *Crisis Economics: A Crash Course in the Future of Finance.* London: Penguin.

Sands, Philippe. 2003. *Principles of International Environmental Law.* Cambridge: Cambridge University Press.

Santarius, Tilman. 2007. "Klimawandel und globale Gerechtigkeit." *Aus Politik und Zeitgeschichte* 24:18–24.

Sassen, Saskia. 1996. *Losing Control? Sovereignty in an Age of Globalization.* New York: Columbia University Press.

Scharpf, Fritz W. 1997. "Grenzerfahrung und Grenzüberschreitungen: Demokratie im integrierten Europa." In *Regieren in entgrenzten Räumen,* edited by Beate Kohler-Koch. Opladen: Westdeutscher Verlag.

Schmitt, Carl. 2008. *Land und Meer: Eine weltgeschichtliche Betrachtung.* Stuttgart: Klett-Cotta.

Schmitter, Philippe. 1999. "The Future of Democracy: Could It Be a Matter of Scale?" *Social Research* 66:933–958.

———. 2000. *How to Democratize the European Union . . . and Why Bother?* Oxford: Rowman and Littlefield.

Schudson, Michael. 1999. *The Good Citizen: A History of American Civic Life.* Cambridge, Mass.: Harvard University Press.

Schumpeter, Joseph. 1942. *Capitalism, Socialism and Democracy.* New York: Harper.
Senge, Peter. 1990. *The Fifth Discipline.* New York: Doubleday.
Serfati, Claude. 2009. *Une économie politique de la sécurité.* Paris: Karthala.
Shaw, Martin. 1996. *Civil Society and Media Global Crisis.* London: Pinter.
Skidelsky, Robert. 2009. *Keynes: The Return of the Master.* New York: Public Affairs.
Slaughter, Anne-Marie. 2004. *A New World Order.* Princeton: Princeton University Press.
Sloterdijk, Peter. 1998. *Sphären I: Blasen.* Frankfurt: Suhrkamp.
———. 2005. *Im Weltinnenraum des Kapitals.* Frankfurt: Suhrkamp.
Stern, Nicholas. 2007. *The Economics of Climate Change.* Cambridge: Cambridge University Press.
Stiglitz, Joseph. 2010. *Freefall: America, Free Markets, and the Sinking of the World Economy.* New York: Norton.
Strange, Susan. 1996. *Retreat of the State: The Diffusion of Power in the World Economy.* Cambridge: Cambridge University Press.
Sunstein, Cass R. 2005. *Laws of Fear: Beyond the Precautionary Principle.* Cambridge: Cambridge University Press.
Swaan, Abram de. 1993. *Der sorgende Staat: Wohlfahrt, Gesundheit und Bildung in Europa und den USA der Neuzeit.* Frankfurt: Campus.
Thompson, Janice E. 1994. *Mercenaries, Pirates and Sovereigns: State-Building and Extraterritorial Violence in Early Modern Europe.* Princeton: Princeton University Press.
Thucydides. 1972. *The History of the Peloponnesian War.* Edited by M. I. Finley. Translated by Rex Warner. London: Penguin.
Tönnies, Ferdinand. (1887) 1960. *Gemeinschaft und Gesellschaft.* Darmstadt: Wissenschaftliche Buchgesellschaft.
United States Department of the Treasury. 2009. "Financial Regulatory Reform: A New Foundation." www.financialstability.gov/roadtostability/regulatoryreform.html.
Vaidhyanathan, Siva. 2011. *The Googlization of Everything (And Why We Should Worry).* Berkeley: University of California Press.
Walker, Rob B. J. 1993. *Inside/Outside: International Relations as Political Theory.* Cambridge: Cambridge University Press.

Weiler, Joseph. 1999. *The Constitution of Europe*. Cambridge: Cambridge University Press.

Weizman, Eyal. 2007. *Hollow Land: Israel's Architecture of Occupation*. London: Verso.

Welzer, Harald. 2007. *Klimakriege: Wofür im 21. Jahrhundert getötet wird*. Frankfurt: Fischer.

Wildavsky, Aaron. 1988. *Searching for Safety*. New Brunswick, N.J.: Transaction Books.

Wilhelm, Anthony G. 2000. *Democracy in the Digital Age: Challenges to Political Life in Cyberspace*. London: Routledge.

Willke, Helmut. 2007. *Smart Governance: Governing the Global Knowledge Society*. Frankfurt: Campus.

Willke, Helmut, and Gerhard Willke. 2012. *Political Governance of Capitalism: A Reassessment Beyond the Global Crisis*. Cheltenham, UK: Edward Elgar.

Young, Iris Marion. 2010. "Verantwortung und globale Gerechtichkeit: Ein Model sozialer Verbundenheit." In *Globale Gerechtigkeit: Schlüsseltexte zur Debatte zwischen Partikularismus und Kosmopolitismus*, edited by Christoph Broszies and Henning Hahn, 329–369. Frankfurt: Suhrkamp.

Zürn, Michael, and Matthias Ecker-Ehrhardt. 2007. "Die Politisierung internationaler Institutionen." *Aus Politik und Zeitgeschichte* 20–21:24–30.

———. 2012. *Die Politisierung der Weltpolitik*. Berlin: Suhrkamp.

Zürn, Michael, and Gregor Waiter-Drop. 2011. "Democracy and Representation Beyond the Nation State." In *The Future of Representative Democracy*, edited by Sonia Alonso, John Keane, and Wolfgang Merkel, 258–281. Cambridge: Cambridge University Press.

INDEX

advanced nations, and climate change, 125–128, 131–134, 137–139. *See also* Europe; European Union; *and specific nations*
Africa, 126, 127. *See also* Sudan
Agamben, Giorgio, 70–71
Agnew, John, 76
Alien Tort Statute (1789), 27–28
Anders, Günter, 55
antiglobalization, 14
asymmetries: in the causes and impacts of climate change, 125–130; and the demand for inclusion, 47–48; in efforts to stop climate change, 131–135; and fear of the Other, 54–55; of immigration, 171–172; the Internet and, 100–102; the transgression of boundaries, 69
authoritarianism: and emergencies, 66; global fear and, 51; Internet and authoritarian systems, 100, 103–104
autonomy, individual, 16

Balibar, Étienne, 77
Bangladesh, 128
banking, 23–24, 46–47, 148. *See also* financial arena
barriers: and migration, 31–32, 69–70, 73–74; permeability of, 38; wall multiplication, 68–72; wall psychopathology, 72–75. *See also* borders; boundaries
Bauman, Zygmunt, 10, 30, 51, 52, 76
Beck, Ulrich, 29, 35, 60, 160
Benjamin, Walter, 57
besieged societies, 74
biopiracy, 13, 25–26
Bloch, Ernst, 166
Boltanski, Luc, 16
borders: alternative conceptions of, 68; benefits of, 79–80; blurring of, and threats/protections, 36, 77; borderless world, 68–69; flexibility/rigidity of, 73–74, 80; future of, 78–80, 85; historical concepts of territorial borders, 6–7, 75–76; location of, in

borders (*continued*)
  globalized world, 76–77; wall
  multiplication, 68–72; wall
  psychopathology, 72–75. *See
  also* barriers; boundaries;
  immigration; outlying areas,
  world without; territory
boundaries: boundarylessness,
  35 (*see also* interdependence;
  ungoverned spaces); criterion
  for drawing, 48; future of,
  78–80; in global politics,
  76–77; and the new security, 78;
  psychopathology of, 72–75. *See
  also* barriers; borders
Bourke, Joanna, 52
Brown, Wendy, 70

capitalism: governance of global
  capitalism, 146–155; and internet
  piracy, 16; without property,
  17–20. *See also* economic arena;
  financial arena; stock market
carbon emissions, 125–126, 132–133.
  See also climate change
Castells, Manuel, 95
Cayman Islands, 23
Chiapello, Ève, 16
China, 126, 131–132
Cicero, 11–12
cities, 71, 73
citizenship, 28, 179
climate change: as area of
  responsibility, 123; causes and
  impacts, 124–130, 132–133;
  challenges to reaching
  agreement on, 129, 130–131;
  changing perceptions of weather
  and climate, 122–124; climate
  justice and efforts to halt
  climate change, 130–135, 137–138;
  context of, 118; controversy
  over, 123–124; future conflicts
  and migration due to, 124–125;
  global governance of, 135–139;
  international institutions and,
  122; as technological failure, 63
comical, the, 176, 178
commonality: global
  interconnectedness, 40–48;
  sense of shared humanity, 44–45;
  universal exposure to threats,
  33–40. *See also* common good;
  global humanity; identity;
  interdependence; public goods;
  universal exposure; universality
common good, 180–183. *See also*
  public goods
communication, 83–85, 98. *See also*
  Internet
community: and identity, 174, 176,
  182 (*see also* identity); unequal
  protections and, 37
conflict, 124, 155. *See also*
  international intervention
Constitutional Treaty for Europe, 107
consumption, 13, 27
contagious realities, 29, 34–36. *See
  also* interdependence; threats;
  universal exposure

cooperation: climate change and, 129–135, 137–138; disasters and, 155; and financial governance, 47; international agencies and ungoverned spaces, 25; need for, in an interdependent world, 141; and the new security, 78
Copenhagen Accord, 139. *See also* climate change
Critique of Pure Reason (Kant), 7
culture: cultural jamming, 15; diversity, 79; the familiar vs. the unfamiliar, 176–178; immigrants and, 171–173; openness of culture, 165–166; risk perception and response, 60
cyberspace. *See* Internet

Dahl, Robert, 108–109
Declaration of Independence (U.S.), 174–175
Declaration of the Rights of Man and of the Citizen, 18
Deleuze, Gilles, 14, 34
Delmas-Marty, Mireille, 158
Delumeau, Jean, 52
democracy: beyond nations, 105–113; democratic society in an uncertain world, 65–66; democratic vigilance, 83–84, 89–92, 101 (*see also* observation society); fear and, 55–56; financial governance and, 148–149; functional democratization, 130; immediacy and, 88–89;

and international institutions, 105–113; in a knowledge society, 179–180; opacity and, 91, 93–94 (*see also* opacity); as plebiscite, 109; technology and the illusion of democratization, 97–104; transparency and, 88–89
dengue fever, 127
deregulation, 23–24, 96. *See also* regulation
Derrida, Jacques, 37, 166, 174–175
deterritorialization, 26, 27–28, 147. *See also* territory
détournement, 14
developing nations, and climate change, 125–128, 131–135, 137–138. *See also specific nations*
Dewey, John, 45
digital activism, 103–104
diplomacy (public vs. secret), 85, 86, 89–90. *See also* WikiLeaks
disasters, 66, 127–128, 155. *See also* climate change
disease, 127
Durkheim, Émile, 62, 190

economic arena: 1870–1913 era, 142; causes of poverty, 121; climate change and, 124, 135–137; current (global) economic crisis, 23, 46–47, 62, 89, 94–96, 147–148, 151–152; in a gaseous world, 32 (*see also* gaseous world); immigration's economic impact, 169–171;

economic arena (*continued*)
  neofeudalization, 72; opacity in, 94–97 (*see also* opacity); right to monetary interference, 43; systemic economic risks, 150–152; volatility of, 34. *See also* capitalism; financial arena
Economist (magazine), 56
Elias, Norbert, 130
emergencies. *See* disasters; threats
environment. *See* climate change
environmental movement, 65–66
Europe, 126, 132, 171. *See also* European Union; immigration
European Union, 106–112, 138, 139. *See also* Europe
experts: and demands for participation, 48; failures of, 63, 65; financial experts, 97; and novices, 178–180; and risk assessment, 61. *See also* science

failed states, 21–22, 104, 144. *See also* ungoverned spaces
fear: alarmism, 61; and the desire for traceability, 27; functions of, 53–56, 61; "global fear" defined, 51; governing/managing fears, 38–40, 62; of the Other, 36–37, 54–55, 70 (*see also* Other, the); politics and, 54–56, 59–60; precaution and risk aversion, 57–58; rationality of, 52–56; responses to, 36–38, 39, 51; of ungoverned spaces, 22, 24;

universal exposure and, 33–39. *See also* risk(s); threats
financial arena: deregulation of, 23–24, 96; disconnect between commerce, capital, and currency exchange, 31; governance of global capitalism, 146–155; instability in, 34; market self-governance, 154; opacity in, 94–97, 146–147, 148; piracy and pillage in, 14–15; regulation of, 43, 46–47, 150; stocks as property, 19–20. *See also* economic arena
fortifications, 72–73. *See also* walls
Foucault, Michel, 83
Fraser, Nancy, 119
free expression, 102–103
free riders, 4
French Civil Code (1784), 17
Fuchs, Peter, 177
future, the, 185–187. *See also* intergenerational justice

gaseous world, 29–33. *See also* liquid world
Geithner, Timothy, 152
generational injustice, 124, 128, 132–133
generational interdependence, 185–187
genetic appropriation, 13, 25–26
Germany, 65–66, 103, 107–108
Giddens, Anthony, 84, 132
global governance: of capitalism, 146–155; of climate change,

135–139 (*see also* climate change); form or system of, 158–159; and public goods, 145, 155–156, 158; public space and debate in, 84–85; scope and nature of, 45–46; and threat protection/prevention strategies, 39–40. *See also* global public space; politics of humanity

global humanity: construction of universality, 189–191; formation of, as new subject, 86; sense of shared humanity, 44–45; transnational humanism, 105, 113–118. *See also* identity

globalization: ambiguities of, 68, 70; and boundaries/walls, 68–72; challenges of global democratization, 110–111; and common (transnational) issues, 8, 140–141 (*see also* climate change); compared to 1870–1913 era, 141–142; and the current economic crisis, 46–47; democratizing globalization, 47–48, 160; emergence of a global public space, 84–86; fear of, 51; fluidity of, 10–11, 30–32 (*see also* liquid world); and the future of politics, 160 (*see also* global governance; politics of humanity); "gaseous world" metaphor, 29–33; and global justice, 119 (*see also* justice); and identity, 45 (*see also* identity);

and interdependence, 114; Kant and the idea of, 40; and market governance, 146, 147–148 (*see also* capitalism); observational society and, 84–88; states' abilities weakened by, 144; and the tactics of piracy, 5; as world without outlying areas, 40–48, 191

global public space: emergence of, 84–86; limits to transparency in, 88–93

global warming. *See* climate change

"glocalization," 139

Google, 102

Gosse, Philip, 3, 11

Greenhouse Development Rights (GDR), 138. *See also* climate change

Green parties, 65–66

Grotius, Hugo, 8–9

group identity. *See* identity

Guantanamo military prison, 28

Guattari, Félix, 14, 34

Habermas, Jürgen, 108

Held, David, 41, 48, 110

Hill, Christopher, 11

History of Piracy, The (Gosse), 3

Hobbes, Thomas, 8, 10, 42, 53, 54, 77

human body, 38

humanism. *See* transnational humanism

humanitarian aid, 121

humanity, global. *See* global humanity

humanity, politics of. *See* politics of humanity

human rights, 113–114, 116–118, 120. *See also* justice; transnational humanism

identity (the "us"): and the common good, 180–183; community and, 173–175; construction of universality, 189–191; convergence of the us, 187–191; and Derrida's "ghosts," 166; distinction between us and them, 161, 165, 181–182, 191 (*see also* Other, the); epistemology of the "us," 176–180; experts and novices, 178–180; the familiar vs. the unfamiliar, 176–178; historical investigation of, 167–168; locals and immigrants, 169–173; ontology of the "us," 164–175; practice of the "us," 180–187; and proximity (neighbors), 183–184, 186–187; the question of "us," 161–164, 187–189

ignorance and politics, 86–87. *See also* secrecy and secrets

imaginary, the, 53

immigration: barriers/walls and, 31–32, 69–70, 73–74; and citizenship, 28; and cultural exchange, 172–173; economic costs, 169–171; and identity, 169, 171–173. *See also* migration

immunity, 37–38, 41–42. *See also* security; threats

inclusion, demands for, 47–48

India, 69–70, 98, 126, 128, 131–132

inequality, 47–48, 100–102. *See also* asymmetries; justice; Other, the

information: availability of, 89–91, 98, 103; socio-political contexts of, 99–100. *See also* communication; Internet; opacity; transparency

insecurity, culture of, 61–62

inside. *See* interiority and exteriority

intellectual property, 3–4. *See also* biopiracy

interdependence: and climate change, 129–130 (*see also* climate change); and the common good, 182; and contagious realities, 29, 34–36; creating a politics of humanity, 155–157; and democratic responsibility, 111; and the financial crisis, 151–152; and the future of politics, 160 (*see also* politics of humanity); generational interdependence, 185–187; globalization and, 114, 141–143; and global justice, 119 (*see also* justice); logic of, 142; and protection/prevention strategies, 39–40; proximity and, 183 (*see also* proximity); public goods and, 140–146 (*see also* public goods); security and, 141; sovereignty and, 111–116; in a world without outlying areas, 40–48, 191. *See also* commonality

intergenerational justice, 124, 128, 132–33, 185–87
interiority and exteriority: barriers/walls and, 70, 71 (*see also* barriers; borders; boundaries); boundaries vs. nets, 76–77; and financial imbalances, 46–47; world without outlying areas, 40–48, 191
intermediaries, mistrust of, 88
international community, as term, 157
International Criminal Court, 112
international institutions: authority and responsibility of, 106; and climate change, 122; democracy and, 105–113; imperfect structure of, 157. See also *specific institutions*
international intervention, 113–114, 116–117, 119
International Monetary Fund (IMF), 112
international relations, 143–144, 156–157. See also diplomacy
Internet: and democratization and power, 97–104; deregulation and, 24; and individual autonomy, 16; and intellectual property, 4; maritime and pirate metaphors, 15; neutrality of, 102–103; participation enabled by, 93; piracy in, 16; as site of anti-institutional struggle, 15–16; and transparency, 89–93 (*see also* WikiLeaks). See also nets

intersubjectivity, 163–164
Iraq war, 86
Israel, 69–70

Japan, 126
Johns, Adrian, 4
Jonas, Hans, 55
journalism, 88, 92, 93
Joshi, Vijay, 134
Julius, A. J., 119
justice: climatic justice (*see* climate change); global justice, 88, 105, 118–121, 188–189; intergenerational justice, 124, 128, 132–133, 185–187; within nations, 88, 118–119; structural injustice, 120; universal jurisdiction, 117. See also human rights; inequality

Kant, Immanuel, 7, 40
Klein, Naomi, 15
Kluge, Alexander, 185
knowledge society, 5, 150, 152, 179–180. See also Internet; technology
Kyoto Protocol, 131, 138. See also climate change

land. See also territory
land vs. sea, 6–10, 26–27
Lane, Robert E., 63
Latour, Bruno, 35
legitimation, 108–110
Leviathan (Hobbes), 10, 77
Liberia, 23

libertarianism, 15–16
lifeworld, 174
liquid fear, 51
liquid world, 10–11, 26, 30–32, 76. See also gaseous world
loss aversion, 52
Luhmann, Niklas, 163, 177
Luxembourg, 23

Macpherson, Crawford Brough, 18
Margalit, Avishai, 159
Marx, Karl, 98
mediation, 88, 90–93, 102
Melville, Herman, 5, 9
migration: barriers/walls and, 31–32, 69–70; due to climate change, 124–125; favoring, 79. See also immigration
Montesquieu, 177
Morozov, Evgeny, 103
Musil, Robert, 54

nation-state(s). See state(s)
neofeudalization, 72
neoliberalism, 23, 64, 72, 136, 160
Netherlands Antilles, 24
nets, 76–77, 80. See also Internet
NGOs. See nongovernmental organizations
nongovernmental organizations (NGOs), 25, 148–149

Obama, Barack, 103
observation society: and the global public space, 84–88; limits to transparency in, 88–93; observation and power, 83–84; scrutiny of the state, 94–95; secrets and diplomacy in, 85, 86–87; technology and democratic vigilance, 83–84, 89–91, 101 (*see also* Internet)
OECD countries, 125–126. See also Europe; European Union; *and specific countries*
Offe, Claus, 182
opacity: and democracy, 91, 93–94; of the financial system, 94–97, 146–149, 153; and systemic risks, 151
Other, the: exclusion of, 187–188; fear or hatred of, 36–37, 54–55, 70, 166; group identity and, 165; marginalization of, 176; perceived equivalence between otherness and hostility, 74
outlying areas, world without, 40–48, 191
outside. *See* interiority and exteriority

Palan, Ronen, 21
pandemics, 59
Parsons, Talcott, 62
Patel, Urjit R., 134
patriotism, 168
Peace of Westphalia, 36, 143
Persian Letters (Montesquieu), 177
pillage and pillaging, 13, 14–15. See also piracy

piracy, 3–5, 11–14, 25–28. *See also* pillage and pillaging

Plutarch, 10

Pogge, Thomas W., 121

polemic totality, 163

political systems: factors leading to modern system's success, 143–144; functional legitimation of, 109–110; and global fear, 54; need for, 91–92; and the observation society, 83–84, 94–95; and the privileging of property, 17–18. *See also* politics; state(s)

politics: boundaries in global politics, 76–77; democratic vigilance and, 83–84, 91–92; domestic politics and a politics of humanity, 159; environmental movement and, 65–66; and fear, 54–56, 59–60; and financial (market) governance, 33, 146–155 (*see also* capitalism); ignorance and, 86–87; immunopolitics, risks of, 37; internal vs. external, 44; international institutions and, 105–113; Internet and, 103–104; knowledge-based decision-making, 152; mistrust in the political class, 88; piracy as strategy for, 13–14; and public access to information, 89–90; renationalization of, 72; and the return of the state, 64–65; and risk assessment and management, 59–60, 62–67;

and separatism and borders, 36; and society, 175; and technology, 63–67, 109; and threat avoidance, 57; of wall-building, 74–75 (*see also* walls). *See also* diplomacy; political systems; politics of humanity; resistance and protest

politics of humanity, 140–141; creating, 155–156; defining, 191; governance of global capitalism, 146–155; governing delimited spaces, 155–160; interdependent public goods, 140–146

populism, 110

poverty, 121, 127–128, 189

power: and interdependence, 35–36, 115–116; and international intervention, 113, 116; the Internet and, 99–102; and observation, 83–84 (*see also* observation society); sovereignty exchanged for, 145; states' loss of, 148; suspicion toward, 94; territorial vs. extraterritorial, 75–76. *See also* politics; state(s)

precaution, 57–58. *See also* fear; risk(s); security

progress, 56–57

property, 17–20. *See also* intellectual property

protections. *See* risk(s); security; threats

proximity, 183–184, 186–187

public goods: constructing a world of, 43–48; as fundamental

public goods (*continued*)
  problems of today, 140–141;
  interdependent public goods, 140–146; management of, 5–6, 48; the market and, 135–137; and the need for global governance, 155–156, 158; piracy and, 26; states and, 43, 143–145; triangle of publicness, 142–143. *See also* climate change; common good
public space. *See* global public space
Pulcini, Elena, 52

Rawls, John, 119, 121
refugees, 124–125. *See also* migration
regulation: as attempt to reterritorialize a liquid world, 26–27; better regulation of global market, 150; deregulation, 23–24, 96; environmental protections, 65–66; in a gaseous world, 32–33; ineffectiveness of banking regulations, 46–47; of international credit market, 43; liquidity metaphor and, 30–31; new regulations needed, 26; piracy as indication of lack of, 25–26; technological risks and, 64–65
resistance and protest, 13–14. *See also* politics
responsibility: and climate change, 123, 126, 131–135; difficulty of externalizing, in global world, 42; and European federalization, 110–111; and financial governance, 153–155; for the future, 185–187; imposed on principle of autonomy, 145; interdependence and, 111, 113–115; and international intervention, 113–114, 116–117; of justice, 120 (*see also* justice); for the other and the world, 56; in search of lost responsibility, 25–28; of states, 115
rights, universality of, 28
risk(s): balancing security with, 61–62; climate change, universal/asymmetric risks of, 125–130; cooperation encouraged by understood risks, 155; cultural responses to, 60; democracy and, 65–66; global risks and interdependence, 145–146; governing global risks, 56–62; subjective perception of, 60; systemic economic risks, 150–152; technological failures, 63–64; unpredictability and uncertainty, 33–34, 53–54, 60. *See also* climate change; fear; security; threats
Robin, Corey, 52
Roman Empire, 6–7
Roosevelt, Franklin D., 55
Russia, 18, 31, 129. *See also* Soviet Union
Rwanda, 113

Schmitt, Carl, 7–8, 66, 70–71
science, 57, 63, 179. *See also* technology
sea: contemporary shipping

Index ❦ 213

and jurisdiction over, 11; epistemological meanings of, 6; imperial politics and, 5; vs. land, 6–10; as metaphor, 10, 27 (*see also* liquid world); sea level rise, 128; sovereignty and territorialism and, 7–10
secrecy and secrets, 85–86, 89–90. *See also* ignorance; opacity; transparency
security: balancing risk with, 61–62; as extraterritorial issue, 77; and fear, 52–53; fortifications and, 72–75 (*see also* walls); interdependence and, 141; old vs. new security, 75–78; paradoxes of immunity, 37–38; post-9/11 security policies (U.S.), 77; prevention and its risks/costs, 58–59, 61; states challenged as provider of, 144; unequal protections, 37. *See also* risk(s); threats
separatism, 36
Shaw, Martin, 41
siege mentality, 74
Sloterdijk, Peter, 31
Smith, Adam, 148–149
social programs, 170
social systems, 154, 176–177. *See also* identity
sovereignty: absolute nature of, 114–116, 148; and climate change, 137; exchanged for power, 145; failed states and, 21–22; and human rights, 113–114, 116–118; in an interdependent world, 111–112; and international institutions, 112–113; piracy in opposition to, 11–12; and public goods, 143–145; and responsibility and interdependence, 113–116, 156–157; and the seas, 8–10; state sovereignty uncertain, 24–25, 158; virtual spaces of finance and information and, 22–23; wall-building and, 73 (*see also* boundaries). *See also* state(s)
Soviet Union, 87. *See also* Russia
Srebenica, 113
state(s): authoritarian states, 100, 103–104; and collective goods, 43; and the concepts of border, territory, 6–7, 75–76; as context for justice, 118–119; cooperation instead of competitiveness between, 156–157; cyberspace and, 24; detention by, 28; failed states, 21–22, 104, 144; and financial governance, 47, 146–147, 148, 152–153; as functional and regulatory space, 22; functions of, 143–144, 148–149, 153–154, 156; and global justice, 118–121; and a global public space, 85–86; governing/managing fears, 62; internal order and external chaos, 42; as international actors, 87 (*see also* diplomacy); and international institutions,

state(s) (*continued*) 106–109; and international relations, 143–144, 156; observation (scrutiny) of, 94–95; and the privileging of property, 17–18; and public goods, 143–145; and the question of "us", 188–189; and the seas, 7–10, 11; sovereignty and interdependence and, 113–115, 156–157; state sovereignty uncertain, 24–25; suspicion toward, 94; technological risks and the return of, 64–65; and the value of ignorance, 86–87; wall-building by, 69–71, 74–75 (*see also* walls); warnings issued by, 58; weakening of, 70–71, 158, 188. *See also* political systems; politics; power; sovereignty; ungoverned spaces

Stern Review, 124, 126

stock market, 19–20

Sudan, 125

sustainable development, 57

tax havens, 14–15, 26–27

technology: and democratic vigilance, 83–84, 89–91, 101; and distributed intelligence, 179–180; and global fear, 54; politics and, 63–67, 109; precaution about, 57, 63, 66–67; and social utopia, 97–99. *See also* Internet

territory, 6–10, 75–77. *See also* deterritorialization; sea; walls

terrorism, 12, 22, 33, 74, 77

threats: alerts, 57–58; handling of, in a democratic society, 66; indeterminate threats, 33–34; interdependence and excessive exposure to, 34–36; nonconventional (new) threats, responses to, 78; prevention and its risks/costs, 58–59, 61; responses to fear of, 36–38, 39, 51; and a sense of shared humanity, 44–45; universal exposure, 33–40; unpredictability of, 33–34, 53–54. *See also* fear; immunity; risk(s); security

Thucydides, 6

time. *See* intergenerational justice

Tönnies, Ferdinand, 174

totality, polemic, 163

traceability, 27

transnational humanism, 105, 113–118, 189, 190. *See also* global humanity; politics of humanity

transnational organizations, 44. *See also* nongovernmental organizations

transparency, 88–93, 146, 147. *See also* opacity; secrecy and secrets

Transparency International, 149

Treasury Department, U.S., 152. *See also* Geithner, Timothy

Treaty of Lisbon, 107–108

uncertainty, 61–62; democracy and, 65–66; of fears, threats, and risks, 53, 60–61; in the financial arena, 96; and the governance of complex systems, 152; over management of public goods, 5; uncertain sovereignty, 24–25. *See also* fear; risk(s); threats; traceability

unemployment, 169–170

ungoverned spaces, 20–25. *See also* Internet; piracy; sea

United Nations, 112, 116–117, 133

United Nations Framework Convention on Climate Change, 131–132

United States: border barriers, 69–70; carbon emissions, 126; and climate change, 132, 138; domestic terrorism, 74; post-9/11 security policies, 77; Treasury Department, 152

universal exposure, 33–40

universality, 28, 189–191. *See also* global humanity; politics of humanity

"us." *See* identity

utopianism, 98–99

Vaidhyanathan, Siva, 102

Valéry, Paul, 167

Virgil, 11

walls: ineffectiveness of, 72–74, 77, 79; multiplication of, 68–72; problems created by, 75; and the prohibition of movement, 69–70, 72; psychology of, 70–75

Weber, Max, 190

WikiLeaks, 85, 89, 93

work, 18–19. *See also* unemployment

World Bank, 112

World Health Organization, 59

World Trade Organization, 112

xenophobia. *See* Other, the

Young, Iris Marion, 120